Standards-Based

LANGUAGE ARTS

Graphic Organizers & Rubrics
for Elementary Students

By Imogene Forte
and Sandra Schurr

Incentive Publications, Inc.
Nashville, Tennessee

Graphics by Joe Shibley and Jennifer J. Streams
Cover by Marta Drayton
Edited by Charlotte Bosarge

ISBN 0-86530-627-3

2   3   4   5   6   7   8   9   10   07   06

PRINTED IN THE UNITED STATES OF AMERICA
www.incentivepublications.com

Table of Contents

SECTION 1:
Directions for Using Graphic Organizers . . . 9

SECTION 2:
Graphic Organizers & Rubrics . . . 30

Appendix . . . 111

Index . . . 127

PREFACE

Recent research studies have confirmed a belief that intuitive teachers have long held germane to classroom success: when students are meaningfully involved in active learning tasks and in the planning and evaluation of their work, they are more enthusiastic about instructional activities, they learn and retain more, and their overall rate of achievement is greater. With the emphasis placed on measurable achievement as an overriding goal driving school system mandates, curriculum, classroom organization, and management (and even instructional practices and procedures), teachers are faced with great challenges. While striving to fulfill societal demands, they must also create and use new instructional strategies, procedures, and teaching methods to meet the diverse needs of students with widely varying backgrounds, interests, and abilities. In the rapidly changing world in which we live, and the growing avalanche of information, elementary language arts teachers are turning to student-centered instruction, active learning strategies, and authentic instruction to capture and hold students' interests and attention, and, consequently, result in increased achievement levels.

GRAPHIC ORGANIZERS

As the body of material to be covered in a given time frame grows more massive and multifaceted, and as content demands on students and teachers multiply, graphic organizers are becoming an important component of elementary language arts programs.

In the information-saturated classroom of today, sorting and making meaningful use of specific facts and concepts is becoming an increasingly important skill. Knowing where to go to find information and how to organize it once it is located is the key to processing and making meaningful use of the information gathered. Graphic organizers can be used to provide visual organization, develop scope and sequence, furnish a plan of action, aid in assessment, clarify points of interest, and/or document a process or a series of events.

The construction and use of graphic organizers encourages visual discrimination and organization, use of critical thinking skills, and meta-cognitive reflection. They can be particularly useful in helping elementary students grasp concepts and skills related to the twelve standards established by the National Council of Teachers of English.

In other instances, a graphic organizer may be developed as a reporting or review exercise or sometimes as a means of self-assessment after knowledge has been acquired. Graphic organizers can become valuable and effective instructional tools. The degree of their effectiveness for both students and teachers is determined by visual clarification of purpose, careful planning, organization, and attention to detail.

RUBRICS

Authentic assessment, as opposed to more traditional forms of assessment, gives both student and teacher a more realistic picture of gains made, facts learned, and information processed for retention. With rubrics, more emphasis is placed on the processing of concepts and information than on the simple recall of information. Collecting evidence from authentic assessment exercises, and taking place in realistic settings over a period of time, provides students and teachers with the most effective documentation of both skills and content mastery. Traditional measurements of student achievement such as written tests and quizzes, objective end-of-chapter tests, and standardized tests play a major role in the assessment picture as well.

The use of standards-based rubrics in elementary grade language arts classes has proven to be an extremely useful means of authentic assessment for helping students maintain interest and evaluate their own progress.

Rubrics are checklists that contain sets of criteria for measuring the elements of a product, performance, or portfolio. They can be designed as a qualitative measure (holistic rubric) to gauge overall performance of a prompt, or they can be designed as a quantitative measure (analytic rubric) to award points for each of several elements in response to a prompt.

Additional benefits from rubrics are that they require collaboration between students and teachers, are flexible and allow for individual creativity, make room for individual strengths and weaknesses, minimize competition, are meaningful to parents, allow for flexible time frames, provide multifaceted scoring systems with a variety of formats, can be sources for lively peer discussions and interaction, can include meta-cognitive reflection provisions which encourage self-awareness and critical thinking, and can help teachers determine final grades that are understood by (and hold meaning for) students.

NATIONAL STANDARDS

These standards-based graphic organizers and rubrics have been designed to provide busy elementary language arts teachers with a bank of resources from which to draw as the need arises. The twelve standards developed by the National Council of Teachers of English and the International Reading Association have been incorporated throughout all activities. For ease in planning, the Planning Matrix on pages 114-116 provides a complete correlation of activities to these standards.

Section 1:
Directions for Using Graphic Organizers

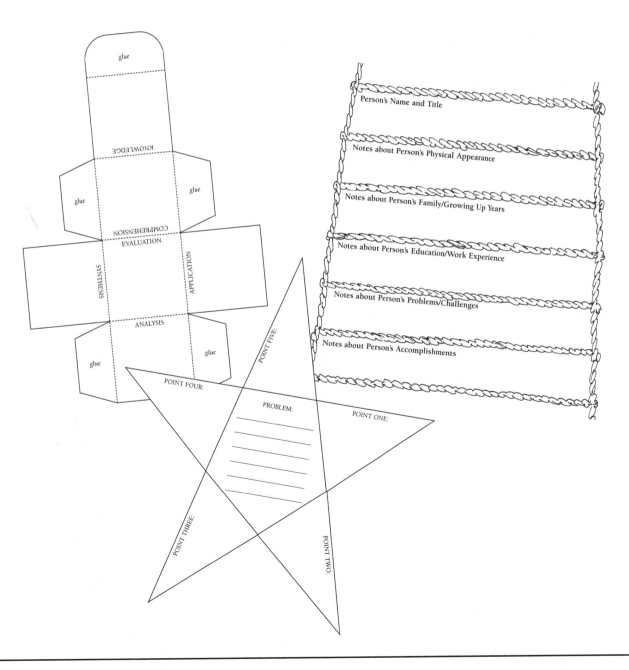

"Any Story" Outline

The "Any Story" outline serves to help students organize their thoughts and develop a cohesive plan for any story they want to write. Once a subject is selected, the "Big Ideas" for the story may be written in the larger headline rectangles.

Two or more "Little Ideas" may then be written under the related "Big Idea." Finally, the headline sections may be numbered from 1 to 5 in the best order for writing the story. This outline may also serve as an organizing tool for collecting ideas for a report on a specific topic requiring use of multiple resources for developing a time line or writing an autobiography.

Reproducible copy may be found on page 31.
Correlated rubric for assessment purposes
may be found on page 32.

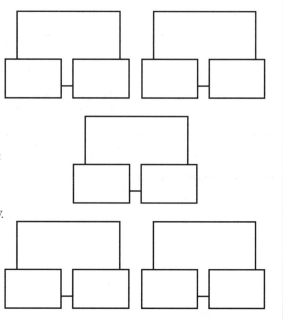

Artist's Rainbow Report

The Artist's Rainbow Report is an organizational tool based on Bloom's Taxonomy of Cognitive Thinking skills to help students organize ideas and information related to the life and work of one specific artist. It will be especially helpful when applied to the illustrations found in a favorite children's book. Organizing thoughts at the six different levels of the taxonomy will encourage critical and systematic thinking, gathering information at the simplest level, and, consequently, following the ascending steps of complexity to complete the report will enable the student to produce a more accurate and creative final product.

For more information related to Bloom's Taxonomy,
see page 122 in the Appendix.

Reproducible copy may be found on page 33.
Correlated rubric for assessment purposes
may be found on page 34.

Author's Life Ladder

The Author's Life Ladder may be used to record important information about an author. It will be used as a tool for organizing data collected from several sources about the life and work of an author of particular interest.

It may also be useful for gathering material for a report on a famous person, media personality, or community leader.

Reproducible copy may be found on page 35. Correlated rubric for assessment purposes may be found on page 36.

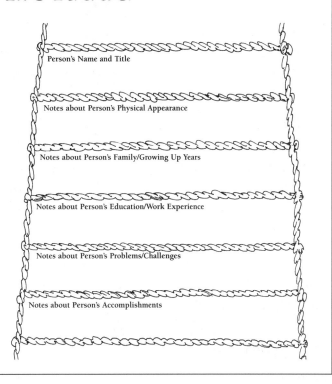

Person's Name and Title

Notes about Person's Physical Appearance

Notes about Person's Family/Growing Up Years

Notes about Person's Education/Work Experience

Notes about Person's Problems/Challenges

Notes about Person's Accomplishments

Autobiography Organizer

The Autobiography Organizer is useful for organizing major facts of a specific life story. It may be used by students as a writing aid for sorting out information and events related to their own lives in preparation for writing their own autobiography. The same graphic organization applies to the study of the biography of a famous person. This is especially true when study allows for use of a variety of resource materials that need to be clarified and coordinated to provide interest, as well as eliminate overlap or redundancy of facts and information.

Reproducible copy may be found on page 37. Correlated rubric for assessment purposes may be found on page 38.

An Autobiography of:	
Place/Date of Birth	
Family History	
Early Life	
Education	
Major Action	
Major Events	
Major Influences	
Major Contributors	
Major Friends	
Major Problems	
Famous Quotes or Words	

Be a Smarty Pants!

Be a Smarty Pants! is a whimsical organizer to help students present thoughts and information in eight different ways. It is based on Howard Gardner's Theory of Multiple Intelligences, which helps teachers and students better understand the way an individual acquires and uses information. Students should be instructed to "show how they are smart" by writing a sentence that tells something about themselves, what they can do, or perhaps how they would do something in each of the blank trouser outlines. Students will then learn more about themselves by reviewing and reflecting on the sentences in order to summarize the information for an "All about Me" report.

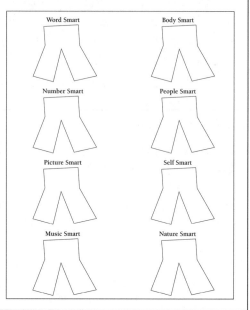

For more information related to Gardner's Multiple Intelligences, see page 121 in the Appendix.

Reproducible copy may be found on page 39. Correlated rubric for assessment purposes may be found on page 40.

Bloom's Taxonomy Book Report Outline

The Bloom's Taxonomy Book Report Outline serves as a valuable tool for students when organizing thoughts about a book they have read.

This outline encourages students to evaluate, synthesize, analyze, apply, comprehend, and become knowledgeable about the material they have read before assembling it into a written, oral, or graphic book report.

For more information related to Bloom's Taxonomy, see page 122 in the Appendix.

Reproducible copy may be found on page 41. Correlated rubric for assessment purposes may be found on page 42.

Title: _____

Author: _____

Publisher: _____ Date: _____

Evaluation

Synthesis

Analysis

Application

Comprehension

Knowledge

Bookmark Homework Helper

The Bookmark Homework Helper will aid students in keeping track and completion of homework assignments. When folded on the dotted line, it may then be decorated on the back with appropriate illustrations to provide interest and motivation or be used for additional teacher instructions or information (examples: math facts, grammar rules, library, or media information, etc.). One of the Bookmark Helper's most attractive features is its adaptability to positioning inside a textbook or student planner. Holes could be punched for a loose-leaf notebook if desired. The format may also be adapted for word lists, unit planning, or ongoing facts or plans for a unit or project.

Reproducible copy may be found on page 43.
Correlated rubric for assessment purposes
may be found on page 44.

Homework for week of	Homework for week of	Homework for week of	Homework for week of
Subject	Subject	Subject	Subject
Assignment	Assignment	Assignment	Assignment
References/ Textbook pages	References/ Textbook pages	References/ Textbook pages	References/ Textbook pages
Due date	Due date	Due date	Due date
Notes	Notes	Notes	Notes
Grade/Teacher Comments	Grade/Teacher Comments	Grade/Teacher Comments	Grade/Teacher Comments
Student's Name	Student's Name	Student's Name	Student's Name

Book Report Pyramid

The Book Report Pyramid can serve as a valuable organizational tool for elementary students of all ages. When properly presented, this organizational procedure encourages critical thinking for material that must be summarized and synthesized in order to fit into the limited spacing, use of plot and sequence, recall selection, and reflection skills.

The same framework may be useful as a planning tool for creative or process writing. It may also be used to develop a report on a biography of a famous person, a factual documentary report of a historical event or social movement, or of a play, movie, or video depicting any of the above. Students should be encouraged to report the facts and important information as accurately as possible, while at the same time employing original illustrations, time lines, story webs, or other details to make the report graphically interesting and informative.

Reproducible copy may be found on page 45.
Correlated rubric for assessment purposes
may be found on page 46.

Name of Book
Author, Publisher, Date
Who (Main Characters)
Where (Setting)
When (Period or Specific Time)
What
Why
How

Bridge of Knowledge Organizer

The Bridge of Knowledge Organizer will be useful as a student planning form for a specific content lesson, a research project, a group unit, or enrichment project. The value of this organizer is the capacity it affords for the entire plan to be shown in a concise manner on one page: topic, plan, resources needed (and their location), student required date of completion, and student and teacher comments.

For more information related to Bloom's Taxonomy, see page 122 in the Appendix.

Reproducible copy may be found on page 47. Correlated rubric for assessment purposes may be found on page 48.

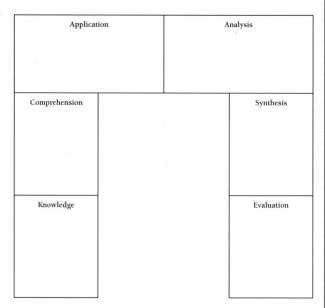

Cause-and-Effect Chain

A series of cause-and-effect relationships, learned from a topic of study or from a book, may be recorded in the appropriate sections of the cause-and-effect chain to review a course of events.

When care is taken to record the events accurately, the chain will show that each cause produces a related effect and that all of the CAUSES lead to the ultimate or final EFFECT.

Reproducible copy may be found on page 49. Correlated rubric for assessment purposes may be found on page 50.

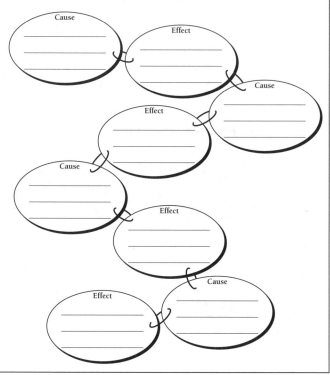

Graphic Organizer

Chalk Talk Organizer

The Chalk Talk Organizer is planned for use by an individual student but may well be expanded to accommodate use by a group. It will be most effective when used as a pre-planning tool and as a guide to efficient project completion. Students should be encouraged to think carefully, to evaluate resources available, and to plan to use the time allotted for the presentation in as creative a manner as possible, always keeping the goal of the "talk" in mind.

This organizer may be found useful in planning other performance tasks with a specific theme and time allotment.

Reproducible copy may be found on page 51.
Correlated rubric for assessment purposes may be found on page 52.

Topic _____
Time allotted for talk _____
_____
Format _____
References _____
_____
Graphics _____
Time line and steps for completion _____
_____
Notes _____
_____
_____
_____
_____
_____
_____
_____

Graphic Organizer

Character Analysis Organizer

A Character Analysis Organizer presents biographical information, the personality traits, actions, and accomplishments of a main or supporting character from a novel, short story, textbook, or a newspaper or magazine article. Important pieces of information are recorded on the outline of the character as a visual record of the person's accomplishments, words, actions, and/or deeds.

Reproducible copy may be found on page 53.
Correlated rubric for assessment purposes may be found on page 54.

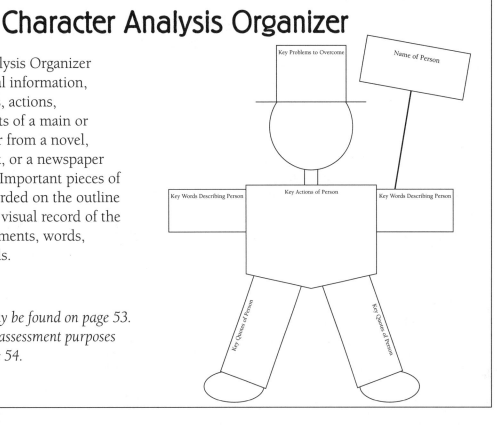

Graphic Organizer

Compare and Contrast Organizer

The Compare and Contrast Organizer is used to relate a newly acquired concept to prior learned knowledge related to the concept. Concept 1 and Concept 2 should be recorded in the two rectangles at the top of the page.

Comparison step: Write how the two concepts are similar in the **How Alike?** box.

Contrast Step: Note the differences between the two concepts in the **How Different?** columns.

Reproducible copy may be found on page 55. Correlated rubric for assessment purposes may be found on page 56.

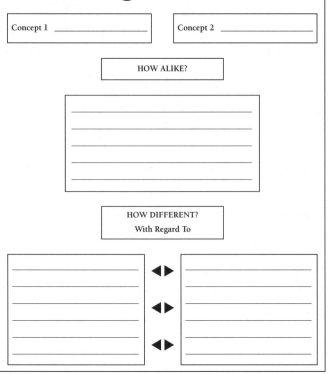

Graphic Organizer

Concept Map

The Concept Map can be especially helpful for showing a series of events from a chapter book, biography, play, or social studies reading assignment. It is built around a central concept important to the study of a given topic. Other facts or insights related to the main idea in some meaningful way are recorded as extensions or associations of the main concept through a series of adjacent lines and circles.

Reproducible copy may be found on page 57. Correlated rubric for assessment purposes may be found on page 58.

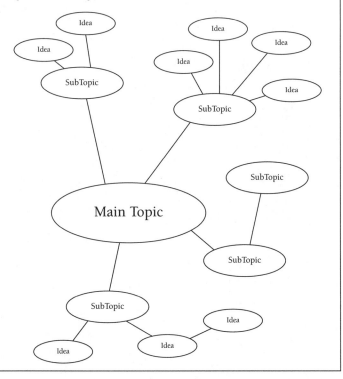

Standards-Based LANGUAGE ARTS
Graphic Organizers & Rubrics for Elementary Students

Crossword or Word Find Puzzle Grid

This grid is used for constructing crossword or word find puzzles for terms for class units or a particular topic.

For a crossword, first make a list of clues for words, then write words in appropriate squares on the grid. Black in the blank squares.

When constructing a word find puzzle, use a separate piece of paper to list words related to a theme or topic. Fill appropriate squares with letters that form these words, then add other letters at random to the blank squares.

Reproducible copy may be found on page 59.
Correlated rubric for assessment purposes
may be found on page 60.

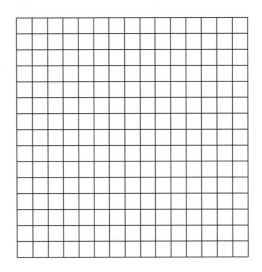

Cube Report Organizer

Since cubes have six sides and information can be recorded on all six sides, the cube report organizer offers a unique format for using Bloom's Taxonomy to organize and present an interesting and informative report. If printed cardboard boxes are used, they should be covered with paper so that the recorded information will be easy to read and study.

There are four steps in developing a cube report: (1) Select a topic. (2) Do research on the topic. Summarize and organize it according to Bloom's Taxonomy. *For information on Bloom's Taxonomy, see page 122.* (3) Construct the cube. (4) Print or type the information on poster or typing paper, and paste the information on the six sides of the cube.

A cube may be made by covering an existing box with butcher paper or wrapping paper, or building a new cube using the pattern provided on page 61. If the second option is selected, enlarge the cube pattern so that the report will be more readable.

Note: The cube lends itself especially well to book reports. When colorful graphics are added, the completed cube makes an interesting art object to remind the reader of an enjoyable reading experience.

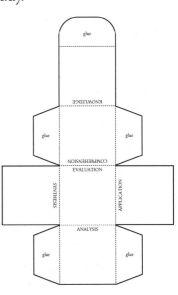

Reproducible copy may be found on page 61.
Correlated rubric for assessment purposes may be found on page 62.

Cycle Organizer

The Cycle Organizer can be used to identify events that tend to be circular or cyclical in nature. The book or topic title or historical event is written in the title circle, then the student writes the events or situations that must (or did) take place in sequential ovals to complete the cycle.

The first event or situation should be recorded at the top circle, with subsequent events recorded in the other circles moving in a clockwise direction. Additional circles may be inserted anywhere in the cycle as needed.

Reproducible copy may be found on page 63. Correlated rubric for assessment purposes may be found on page 64.

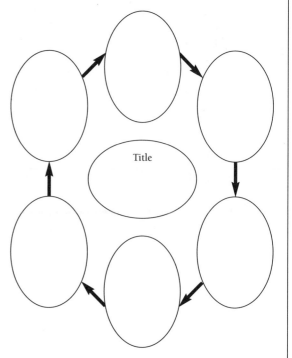

Digging the Dictionary Study Guide

The Digging the Dictionary Study Guide is helpful for developing fluency and proficiency in the use of dictionaries as well as providing practice in the use of alphabetical order and parts of speech.

Using the directions in Column A, the students will use a dictionary to fill in the rest of the graphic organizer.

Reproducible copy may be found on page 65. Correlated rubric for assessment purposes may be found on page 66.

COLUMN A	COLUMN B	COLUMN C
cr — verb		
str — verb		
bl — adjective		
th — noun		
ea — adjective		
cl — adjective		
tr — verb		
fl — noun		
sn — noun		
dr — adjective		
on — adverb		
wr — verb		
ca — noun		
qu — adverb		
fa — verb		
ch — noun		
sp — noun		
gr — adjective		

5 Ws and How Web

The 5 Ws and How Web is used to record the who, what, when, where, why, and how of a magazine article, a newspaper article, or an excerpt from a classroom textbook. The article or chapter titles are written in the center hexagon, and the answers to questions about the situation are written in the appropriate web sections. A paragraph can then be created on a separate page to summarize the information from this web.

Reproducible copy may be found on page 67. Correlated rubric for assessment purposes may be found on page 68.

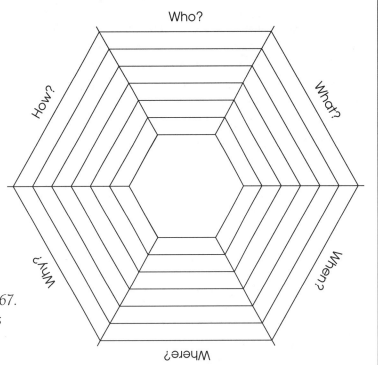

Group Book Report Collage Plan

A Group Book Report Collage Plan can be an interesting alternative for the traditional format most often used for chapter books, biographies, or content-based documentaries. It may be completed by a small group of students who create a mural as a collaborative report, it may be completed by one student as an individual report, or by two students who choose to use it as a product for authentic assessment of a peer tutoring study project. If it is used for a group report, the group decides on a topic, assigns different research tasks to each group member, and cooperatively outlines both the information and the illustrations to be included in the collage. Individuals or peer tutoring teams follow the same procedure with appropriate modifications.

Reproducible copy may be found on page 69. Correlated rubric for assessment purposes may be found on page 70.

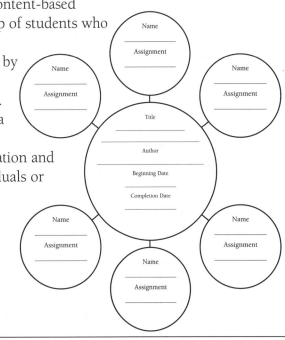

Group Report Mural Organizer

The Group Report Mural Organizer may be used as a planning tool for both group and individual group member use. It may be used to plan a report on a single book read by every member of a given group, culminate a unit of study, cover multiple readings, or as a topical report on an assigned topic. This organizer will be especially useful for including students at varying ability and interest levels with the goal of positive participation of all members of the group.

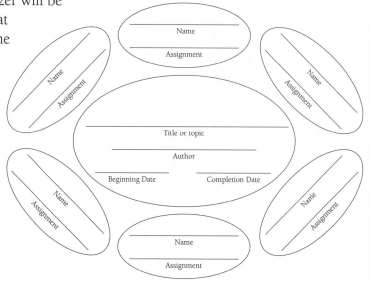

Reproducible copy may be found on page 71.
Correlated rubric for assessment purposes may be found on page 72.

Independent Study Planning Tool

The Independent Study Planning Tool may be used to map out a game plan for completing an independent study of a specific topic, or an author's work, or a current event of particular significance. Since this planning tool is flexible in nature to allow for individual creativity, it is important that details and plans for completing the study be recorded accurately and be very specific in nature.

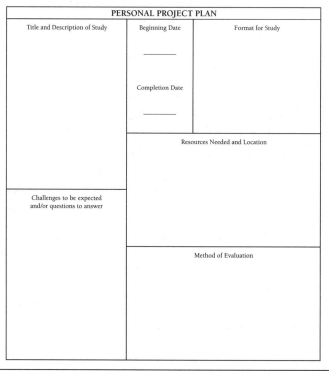

Reproducible copy may be found on page 73.
Correlated rubric for assessment purposes may be found on page 74.

Graphic Organizer

Individual Project Plan Organizer

Use this form to clarify assignments, dates, materials needed, goals, and a plan of action when beginning an individual learning project. While this visual approach to planning can be extremely helpful for many students, it is especially applicable for students with short attention spans and/or under-developed organizational skills. In such circumstances, it can be utilized as a teacher/student planning tool.

Reproducible copy may be found on page 75. Correlated rubric for assessment purposes may be found on page 76.

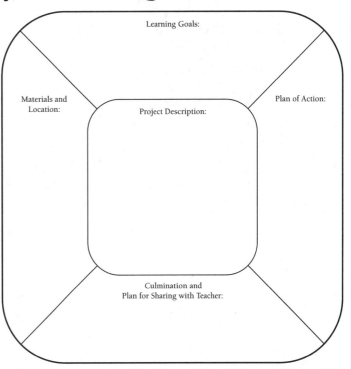

Learning Goals:

Materials and Location:

Project Description:

Plan of Action:

Culmination and Plan for Sharing with Teacher:

Graphic Organizer

Interview Organizer

The Interview Organizer is designed to plan an upcoming interview with a person of interest. It is based on a set of questions asked by the interviewer with spaces provided for recording the interviewee's responses. Answers to the questions may then be used to structure the interview summary or as data for compiling a research report.

Reproducible copy may be found on page 77. Correlated rubric for assessment purposes may be found on page 78.

Getting Ready for the Interview
Name of Interviewee _____
Name of Interviewer _____
Date of Interview _____
Purpose of Interview _____
_____

Conducting the Interview
Question One _____
_____
Response _____

Question Two _____

Response _____

Question Three _____

Response _____

Following the Interview
Results of the Interview _____
_____
_____
_____

Journalist's Template

The sequence of events as presented in the Journalist's Template illustrates the relative importance of the various components of an article written by a journalist. This information and procedure may also be used for creating a television documentary or advertisement. Since news articles must be written immediately after an event occurs in order to appear in print in a timely manner, it is of the utmost importance that the article is written quickly yet accurately. Therefore, the template can be a valuable organizational tool when properly used.

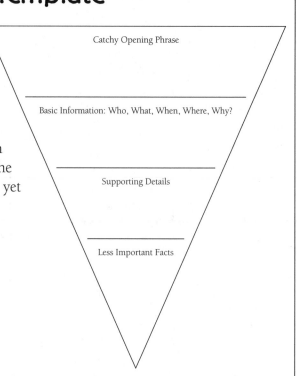

Reproducible copy may be found on page 79. Correlated rubric for assessment purposes may be found on page 80.

Literature Analysis Stairway

By following the steps on the Literature Analysis Stairway, students will be able to analyze the major parts of a short story, novel, or poem. Details, descriptions, events, clue words, traits, attributes, or ideas that summarize elements of the piece of literature may be noted. Notes may be reviewed to help the student construct a definitive statement to summarize the work.

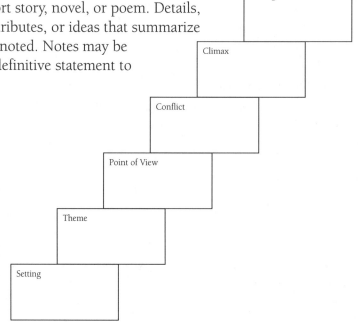

Reproducible copy may be found on page 81. Correlated rubric for assessment purposes may be found on page 82.

Graphic Organizer

Multiple Tasks Planning Guide

The Multiple Tasks Planning Guide is useful as a tool for completing a project based on a major topic and learning goals to be accomplished through the completion of sequentially-ordered tasks. The major goal is written in the large "Topic Title & Description" box, and the "Learning Goals" are written in the medium-sized boxes. Then, the sequence of "Learning Tasks" is organized in the smaller boxes. It is important that each set of tasks be grouped with the appropriate Learning Goal in the diagram.

Reproducible copy may be found on page 83. Correlated rubric for assessment purposes may be found on page 84.

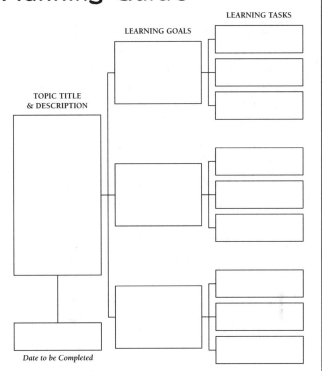

Graphic Organizer

Observation Log

An Observation Log is a collection of simple but informative entries about a given topic or subject. Observation logs are used to guide observation of a person, place, or thing over a period of time and to record the changes describing the observed event or action. Entries include the date and time of the observation in addition to the specific, recorded information.

Date: _____ Time: _____
Observation:_____
_____
_____
_____
_____
_____
_____
_____
_____

Date: _____ Time: _____
Observation:_____
_____
_____
_____
_____
_____
_____
_____
_____

Reproducible copy may be found on page 85. Correlated rubric for assessment purposes may be found on page 86.

Portfolio Planning Guide

The Portfolio Planning Guide contains a collection of artifacts reflecting student interest and efforts related to a designated content discipline or specific topic. It should contain a variety of items of different natures and may include writing samples, photographs, field experiences, reports, interviews, graphics, and both product and performance notes and reflections. Carefully completed, this graphic organizer will serve as a valuable reference tool as well as planning guide.

Reproducible copy may be found on page 87. Correlated rubric for assessment purposes may be found on page 88.

Prediction Web

The Prediction Web is a valuable tool for organizing facts and information to deduce or support a prediction. Write the major topic or problem under discussion as a question in the square box at the bottom of the web. Brainstorm possible predictions or probable outcomes in response to the question and record these in the prediction boxes. On the proof lines, record facts that either support or negate the predictions.

This organizer can be used when studying a current event such as an election, sporting event, decision-making process, etc. Or it may be useful in character analysis of the main character or events in a book or story.

Reproducible copy may be found on page 89. Correlated rubric for assessment purposes may be found on page 90.

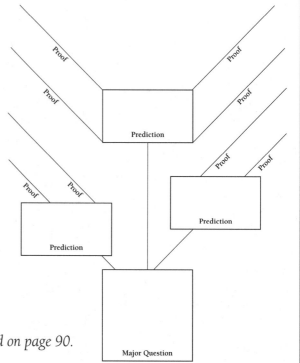

Graphic Organizer

Problem-Solving Star

The Problem-Solving Star encourages students to consider various points or solutions to a specific problem under study. The problem is written in the center of the star and the key points to consider or potential solutions to the problem are written on the five points of the star.

This graphic organizer can be used to gather information for a content-based report, to pinpoint questions resulting from a textbook reading assignment, or to organize main issues and information for a research project.

Reproducible copy may be found on page 91. Correlated rubric for assessment purposes may be found on page 92.

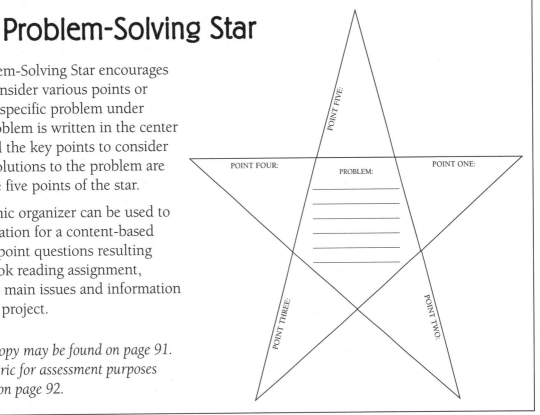

Graphic Organizer

Scope and Sequence Chart

The Scope and Sequence Chart is useful for creating a time line, organizing a sequence of events, or outlining a series of steps to perform a task. In the first box, write the first date, event, or step of the task. In the second box, write the second date, event, or step of the task. Continue this way with the third, fourth, and fifth boxes. Additional boxes may be used if there is need for more stages in the planning process.

Reproducible copy may be found on page 93. Correlated rubric for assessment purposes may be found on page 94.

Historical Setting
Historical Figures
Historical Problem Situation
First Event/Step:
Second Event/Step:
Third Event/Step:
Fourth Event/Step:
Fifth Event/Step:
Outcome(s)
Resolution

*Standards-Based LANGUAGE ARTS
Graphic Organizers & Rubrics for Elementary Students*

SQ3R Chart

The SQ3R Chart is helpful when reading a chapter or section of a textbook or story. SQ3R means survey, question, read, recite, and review.

Survey: Read titles/subtitles. Notice words/phrases in special type. Skim illustrations/charts/graphs. Review end-of-chapter summaries and questions.

Question: Turn main/subtopics in special print into 5W questions—Who, What, When, Where, and Why.

Read: Read information to answer questions, highlight main ideas, and make notes.

Recite: Pause at the end of each chapter section to answer questions orally, using your own words.

Review: Construct a study guide sheet with summaries and main ideas from your reading.

Reproducible copy may be found on page 95. Correlated rubric for assessment purposes may be found on page 96.

Directions to Student:

Use one chart for each major section of the chapter. Remember that SQ3R means:

<u>S</u>urvey: Read titles/subtitles. Notice words/phrases in special type. Skim illustrations/charts/graphs. Review end-of-chapter summaries and questions.

<u>Q</u>uestion: Turn main/subtopics in special print into 5W questions—Who, What, When, Where, and Why.

<u>R</u>ead: Read information to answer questions, highlight main ideas, and make notes.

<u>R</u>ecite: Pause at the end of each chapter section to answer questions orally, using your own words.

<u>R</u>eview: Construct a study guide sheet with summaries and main ideas from your reading.

Survey: Record most important titles and subtitles from major chapter section.

_____
_____
_____
_____

Question: Write Who, What, When, Where, and Why questions for main/subtopics.

_____
_____
_____
_____

Read: Write short answers to five questions from above.

_____
_____
_____
_____

Storyboard Organizer

The Storyboard Organizer is a valuable tool for presenting a sequence of events in chronological order. It is particularly useful for studying a novel, historical event, or geographic exploration.

It can also be helpful for organizing information, ideas, thoughts, or situations based on when and how events occurred, or on their unique application to the topic under investigation.

Reproducible copy may be found on page 97. Correlated rubric for assessment purposes may be found on page 98.

1.	6.
2.	7.
3.	8.
4.	9.
5.	10.

Graphic Organizer

Surfing the Net Organizer

The Surfing the Net Organizer is designed to aid students in locating and using a variety of websites to obtain and organize information related to different genres of literature. As the website for each genre is located, its address is recorded in the specified circle. Each website should be accompanied by descriptive sentences or key words or phrases.

Reproducible copy may be found on page 99. Correlated rubric for assessment purposes may be found on page 100.

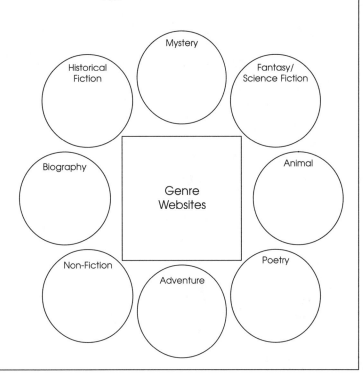

Graphic Organizer

Tall Tale Organizer

Writing a Tall Tale is as easy as A-B-C. With the aid of the Tall Tale Organizer, students can write a 26-line creative tall tale based on each sentence beginning with appropriate letter of the alphabet. The trick is to make each line follow the sequential "train of thought" of the story. After the 26 sentences are completed, the decision can be made as to where to break up the story into at least three paragraphs for a beginning, middle, and end.

Example: "**A**bout 200 years ago, two families wanted to move West. **B**eginning a midnight departure, the families joined together to make this dangerous trip. **C**overed wagons were loaded with supplies and the journey to this new part of the country . . ."

This organizer will really get the creative juices flowing!

Reproducible copy may be found on page 101. Correlated rubric for assessment purposes may be found on page 102.

A . . .	N . . .
B . . .	O . . .
C . . .	P . . .
D . . .	Q . . .
E . . .	R . . .
F . . .	S . . .
G . . .	T . . .
H . . .	U . . .
I . . .	V . . .
J . . .	W . . .
K . . .	X . . .
L . . .	Y . . .
M . . .	Z . . .

Topic Tree Organizer

Use the Topic Tree Organizer to record information and structure your ideas on a topic on any content area. The major topic is written in the oval at the top of the tree, sub-headings in the smaller ovals, and facts and information on the diagonal lines extending from the sub-headings. This graphic organizer is especially useful for organizing and making meaningful use of a vast and unwieldy amount of information on a given subject.

Reproducible copy may be found on page 103. Correlated rubric for assessment purposes may be found on page 104.

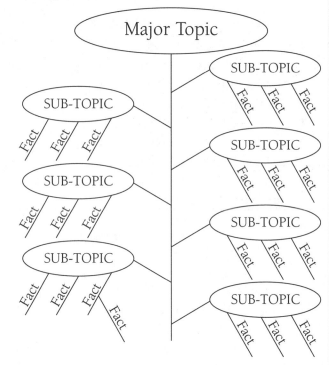

Umbrella Organizer

The Umbrella Organizer is especially helpful for organizing thoughts and ideas for a topical report or essay. The main idea or concept is written inside the umbrella outline in three sentences or less. Then, on the lines adjacent to the handle, details or related thoughts are written. These may be prioritized in some way, such as listing the major details on one side of the handle and the minor details on the other side of the handle. Or, the ideas can be numbered to show priority from most important to least important. This organizer is also useful to evaluate the "pros" and "cons" of a decision.

Reproducible copy may be found on page 105. Correlated rubric for assessment purposes may be found on page 106.

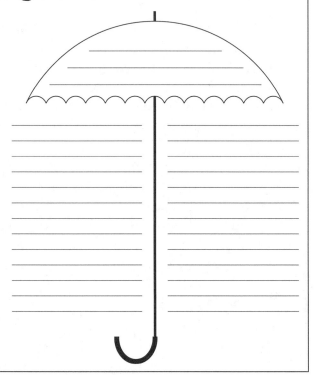

Graphic Organizer

Vocabulary Learning Ladder

The Vocabulary Learning Ladder is useful in helping students learn new words that they discover in their textbooks or other reading. On each step of the ladder, a new word is written, accompanied by the sentence in which the word was found, and the definition of the word.

The tool is especially valuable in encouraging students to develop appreciation for words and extend their vocabularies.

Reproducible copy may be found on page 107. Correlated rubric for assessment purposes may be found on page 108.

Word or Term:_____
Textbook Sentence:_____
Page: ____ Definition: _____
5

Word or Term:_____
Textbook Sentence:_____
Page: ____ Definition: _____
4

Word or Term:_____
Textbook Sentence:_____
Page: ____ Definition: _____
3

Word or Term:_____
Textbook Sentence:_____
Page: ____ Definition: _____
2

Word or Term:_____
Textbook Sentence:_____
Page: ____ Definition: _____
1

Graphic Organizer

What, So What, Now What? Chart

The What, So What, Now What? Chart organizes facts and provides meta-cognitive reflection related to the reading of a story, textbook section, newspaper, or magazine article on a topic.

The What? column requires the student to record a response to the question: What is the meaning of this piece and/or what did I learn from it?

The So What? column requires the student to record a series of responses to the question: What difference does it make now that I know this, or what is its importance?

The Now What? column asks students to record an answer to the question: How can I use this information to make a difference in what I know or can do, or how is it important and relates to the major theme?

Reproducible copy may be found on page 109. Correlated rubric for assessment purposes may be found on page 110.

Topic of Study/Title _____

Student's Name _____

What?	So What?	Now What?

Standards-Based LANGUAGE ARTS
Graphic Organizers & Rubrics for Elementary Students

Section 2:
Graphic Organizers & Rubrics

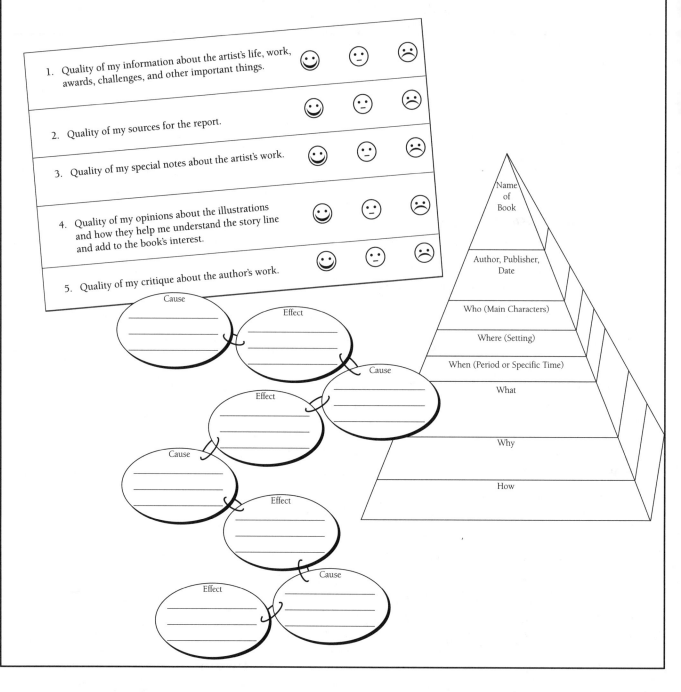

1. Quality of my information about the artist's life, work, awards, challenges, and other important things.

2. Quality of my sources for the report.

3. Quality of my special notes about the artist's work.

4. Quality of my opinions about the illustrations and how they help me understand the story line and add to the book's interest.

5. Quality of my critique about the author's work.

Cause

Effect

Cause

Effect

Cause

Effect

Cause

Effect

Name of Book

Author, Publisher, Date

Who (Main Characters)

Where (Setting)

When (Period or Specific Time)

What

Why

How

"Any Story" Outline

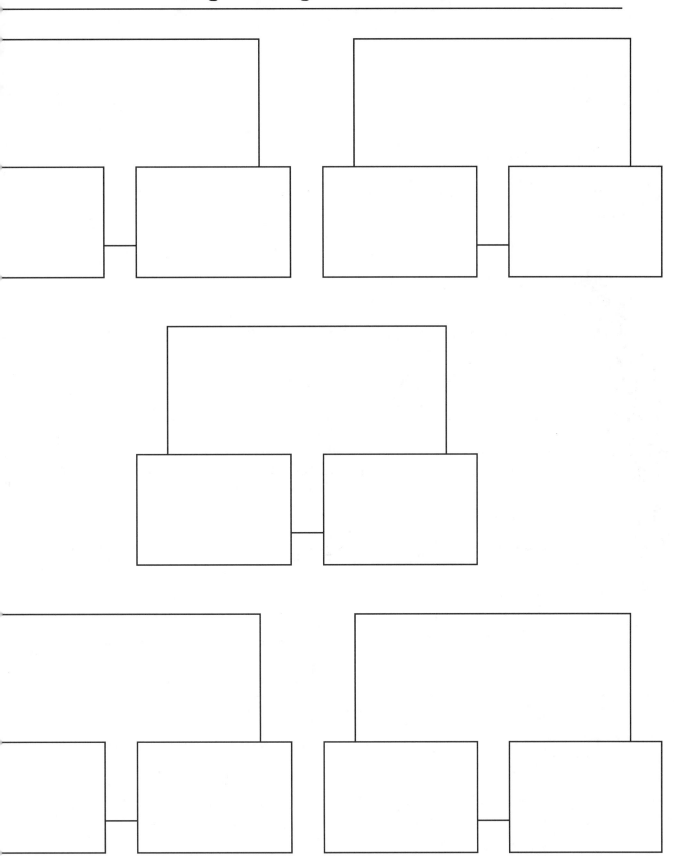

Standards-Based LANGUAGE ARTS
Graphic Organizers & Rubrics for Elementary Students

"Any Story" Outline

Rubric

Rating Scale: 1 Bad News   2 So-So News   3 Great News

Directions to Student:

In the box at the end of each line, write the number that best describes your work.

1. I liked my story topic. ☐

2. I put my big ideas in the headline rectangles. ☐

3. I was able to think of at least 1 or 2 little ideas for each headline. ☐

4. I arranged my big ideas in a logical order that makes sense both to me and my readers. ☐

5. I thought of a good title for my story. ☐

Comments by Student: _____

_____

_____

_____

Signed _____ Date _____

Comments by Teacher: _____

_____

_____

_____

Signed _____ Date _____

Standards-Based LANGUAGE ARTS
Graphic Organizers & Rubrics for Elementary Students

Artist's Rainbow Report

Graphic Organizer

1. Artist

   Date of Birth _____

   Place of Birth _____

   Title of Book in which work appears

   _____

2. Sources used for report _____

   _____

   Special notes about artist's work _____

   _____

3. How the illustrations contribute to the book's attractiveness _____

   _____

4. Artist's other works, awards, honors, challenges _____

   _____

5. High points of artist's life, goals, awards, history _____

   _____

6. Evaluation of Author's work (by critics and/or by me) _____

   _____

   _____

   _____

Standards-Based LANGUAGE ARTS
Graphic Organizers & Rubrics for Elementary Students

Artist's Rainbow Report

Rubric

Rating Scale:

Rainbow Report!   Clouds Gathering   Rain

Directions to Student:

Circle the graphic that best describes your work in each of the areas below.

1. Quality of my information about the artist's life, work, awards, challenges, and other important things.

2. Quality of my sources for the report.

3. Quality of my special notes about the artist's work.

4. Quality of my opinions about the illustrations and how they help me understand the story line and add to the book's interest.

5. Quality of my critique about the author's work.

Comments by Student: _____

_____

_____

Signed _____ Date _____

Comments by Teacher: _____

_____

_____

Signed _____ Date _____

Standards-Based LANGUAGE ARTS
Graphic Organizers & Rubrics for Elementary Students

Copyright ©2004 by Incentive Publications, Inc.
Nashville, TN.

Author's Life Ladder

Graphic Organizer

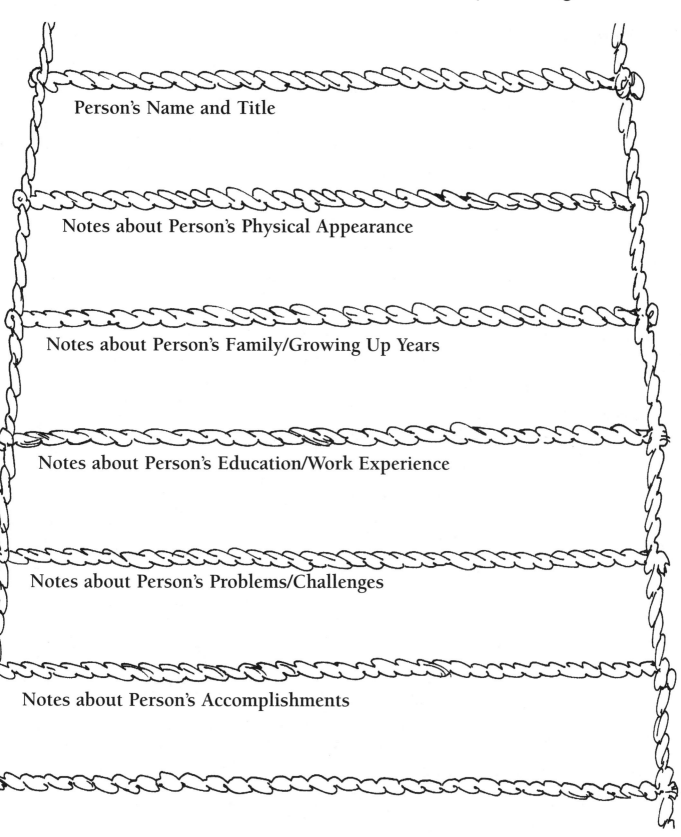

Person's Name and Title

Notes about Person's Physical Appearance

Notes about Person's Family/Growing Up Years

Notes about Person's Education/Work Experience

Notes about Person's Problems/Challenges

Notes about Person's Accomplishments

Standards-Based LANGUAGE ARTS
Graphic Organizers & Rubrics for Elementary Students

Author's Life Ladder

Rubric

Rating Scale:

1	2	3
I did great!	I did all right!	I need to do better!

Directions to Student:

In the box at the end of each line, write in the number that best describes your work on this activity.

1. I learned some things about the author's physical appearance.	☐
2. I learned some things about the author's family and "growing up" years.	☐
3. I learned some things about the author's education.	☐
4. I learned some things about the author's work experiences.	☐
5. I learned some things about the author's personal problems.	☐
6. I learned some things about the author's special challenges.	☐
7. I learned some things about the author's accomplishments.	☐

Comments by Student: _____

_____

_____

Signed _____ Date _____

Comments by Teacher: _____

_____

_____

Signed _____ Date _____

Standards-Based LANGUAGE ARTS
Graphic Organizers & Rubrics for Elementary Students

Copyright ©2004 by Incentive Publications, Inc.
Nashville, TN.

Autobiography Organizer

An Autobiography of:	
Place/Date of Birth	
Family History	
Early Life	
Education	
Major Action	
Major Events	
Major Influences	
Major Contributors	
Major Friends	
Major Problems	
Famous Quotes or Words	

Autobiography Organizer

Rubric

Rating Scale: Great   Fair   Needs Work
              ! ! !   ! !   !

Directions to Student:

In the box at the end of each line, draw in the number of exclamation marks that best describes your work on this activity.

1. I did a good job of writing about the person's family history.	
2. I did a good job of writing about the person's early life.	
3. I did a good job of writing about the person's education.	
4. I did a good job of writing about the person's major actions and activities.	
5. I did a good job of writing about the important events in the person's life.	
6. I did a good job of writing about the person's major contributions.	
7. I did a good job of writing about the person's major friends.	
8. I did a good job of writing about the person's major problems.	
9. I did a good job of writing down some famous words or quotes said by the person.	

Comments by Student: _____

_____

Signed _____ Date _____

Comments by Teacher: _____

_____

Signed _____ Date _____

Standards-Based LANGUAGE ARTS
Graphic Organizers & Rubrics for Elementary Students

Be a Smarty Pants!

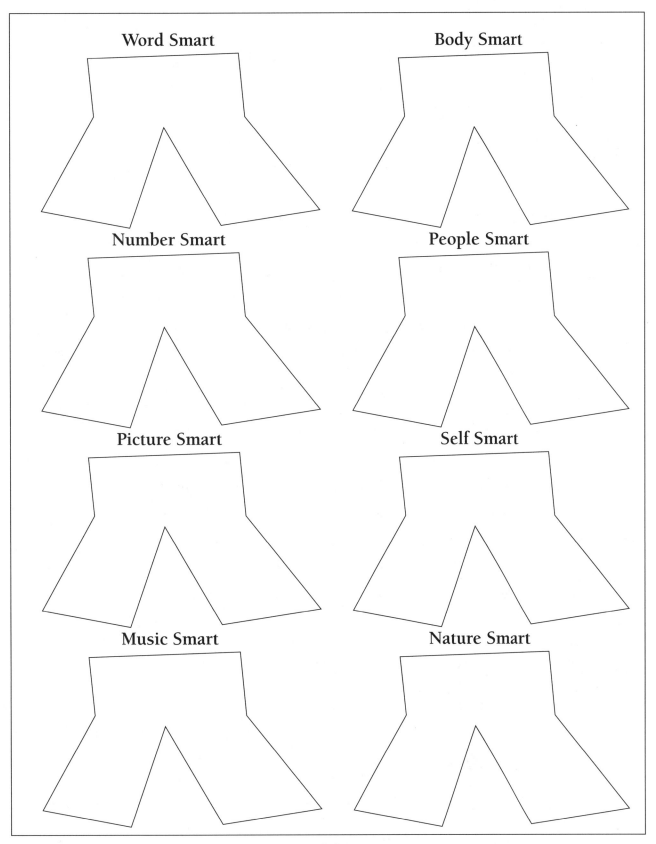

Word Smart

Body Smart

Number Smart

People Smart

Picture Smart

Self Smart

Music Smart

Nature Smart

Standards-Based LANGUAGE ARTS
Graphic Organizers & Rubrics for Elementary Students

Be a Smarty Pants!

Rubric

Rating Scale:

1	2	3
Smart	Smarter	Smartest

Directions to Student:

In the box at the end of each line, write the number that best describes your work on this activity.

1. I was able to write a sentence that shows I am "word smart."	☐
2. I was able to write a sentence that shows I am "number smart."	☐
3. I was able to write a sentence that shows I am "picture smart."	☐
4. I was able to write a sentence that shows I am "music smart."	☐
5. I was able to write a sentence that shows I am "body smart."	☐
6. I was able to write a sentence that shows I am "people smart."	☐
7. I was able to write a sentence that shows I am "self smart."	☐
8. I was able to write a sentence that shows I am "nature smart."	☐

Comments by Student: _____

_____

Signed _____ Date _____

Comments by Teacher: _____

_____

Signed _____ Date _____

Standards-Based LANGUAGE ARTS
Graphic Organizers & Rubrics for Elementary Students

Copyright ©2004 by Incentive Publications, Inc.
Nashville, TN.

Bloom's Taxonomy Book Report Outline

Graphic Organizer

Title: _____

Author: _____

Publisher: _____ Date: _____

Evaluation

Synthesis

Analysis

Application

Comprehension

Knowledge

Standards-Based LANGUAGE ARTS
Graphic Organizers & Rubrics for Elementary Students

Bloom's Taxonomy Book Report Outline

Rubric

Rating Scale:
READY ▷ Needs More Work   SET ▷ Fair   GO ▷ Great

Directions to Student:

Rate your work by writing the words READY, SET, or GO on each blank flag.

1. I worked hard on the Knowledge Level task.	▷
2. I worked hard on the Comprehension Level task.	▷
3. I worked hard on the Application Level task.	▷
4. I worked hard on the Analysis Level task.	▷
5. I worked hard on the Synthesis Level task.	▷
6. I worked hard on the Evaluation Level task.	▷

Comments by Student: _____

_____

_____

_____

Signed _____ Date _____

Comments by Teacher: _____

_____

_____

_____

Signed _____ Date _____

Standards-Based LANGUAGE ARTS
Graphic Organizers & Rubrics for Elementary Students

Bookmark Homework Helper

Graphic Organizer

Homework for week of	Homework for week of	Homework for week of	Homework for week of
Subject	Subject	Subject	Subject
Assignment	Assignment	Assignment	Assignment
References/ Textbook pages	References/ Textbook pages	References/ Textbook pages	References/ Textbook pages
Due date	Due date	Due date	Due date
Notes	Notes	Notes	Notes
Grade/Teacher Comments	Grade/Teacher Comments	Grade/Teacher Comments	Grade/Teacher Comments
Student's Name	Student's Name	Student's Name	Student's Name

Standards-Based LANGUAGE ARTS
Graphic Organizers & Rubrics for Elementary Students

Bookmark Homework Helper

Directions to Student:

Place an "X" in the appropriate box.

	YES	NO
1. I have recorded the appropriate subject on the bookmark.		
2. I have recorded the appropriate assignment on the bookmark.		
3. I have recorded the appropriate references/textbook pages on the bookmark.		
4. I have recorded the appropriate due date on the bookmark.		
5. I have recorded the appropriate notes on the bookmark.		
6. I have recorded the appropriate grade/teacher comments on the bookmark.		
7. I have recorded my name on the bookmark.		

Comments by Student: _____

_____

_____

_____

Signed _____ Date _____

Comments by Teacher: _____

_____

_____

_____

Signed _____ Date _____

Book Report Pyramid

Graphic Organizer

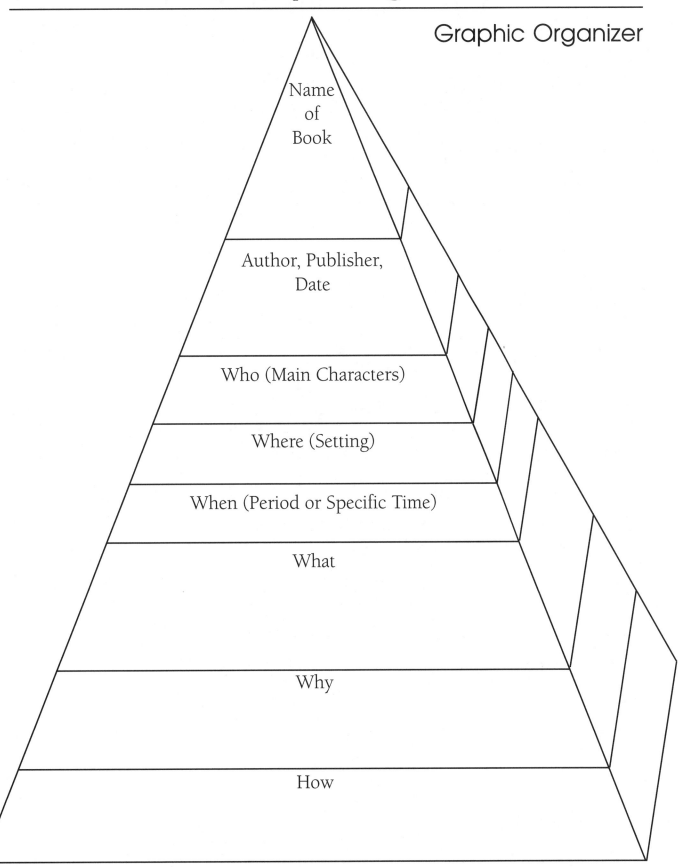

Name
of
Book

Author, Publisher,
Date

Who (Main Characters)

Where (Setting)

When (Period or Specific Time)

What

Why

How

Standards-Based LANGUAGE ARTS
Graphic Organizers & Rubrics for Elementary Students

Book Report Pyramid

Rubric

Rating Scale: Needs Work   Good   Excellent

Directions to Student:

Fill in the pyramid at the end of each line to the level that best describes your work on your book report.

1. I have recorded the name of the BOOK, AUTHOR, PUBLISHER, and COPYRIGHT DATE of the book.	
2. I have described the WHO or main characters in the book.	
3. I have described the WHERE or setting of the book.	
4. I have described the WHEN or specific time period of the book.	
5. I have described the WHAT or plot and sequence of important events in the book.	
6. I have described the WHY or key reasons why things turned out the way they did in the book.	
7. I have described the HOW or the outcome of what happened at the end of the book.	

Comments by Student: _____

_____

_____

Signed _____ Date _____

Comments by Teacher: _____

_____

_____

Signed _____ Date _____

Standards-Based LANGUAGE ARTS
Graphic Organizers & Rubrics for Elementary Students

Copyright ©2004 by Incentive Publications, Inc.
Nashville, TN.

Bridge of Knowledge Organizer

Application	Analysis

Comprehension		Synthesis
Knowledge		Evaluation

Topic _____

Resources Needed _____

Resource Location _____

Completion Date _____

Student Signature: _____ Date: _____

Teacher Signature: _____ Date: _____

Standards-Based LANGUAGE ARTS
Graphic Organizers & Rubrics for Elementary Students

Bridge of Knowledge Organizer

Directions to Student:

Write a simple progress statement in each rectangle that gives an update on how you are coming along on your project/unit plan.

5 Knowledge Level Work

My Update:

4 Synthesis Level Work

My Update:

6 Evaluation Level Work

My Update:

3 Comprehension Level Work

My Update:

7 Topic Chosen

My Update:

2 Analysis Level Work

My Update:

8 Resources Needed

My Update:

1 Application Level Work

My Update:

9 Resource Location

My Update:

Cause-and-Effect Chain

Graphic Organizer

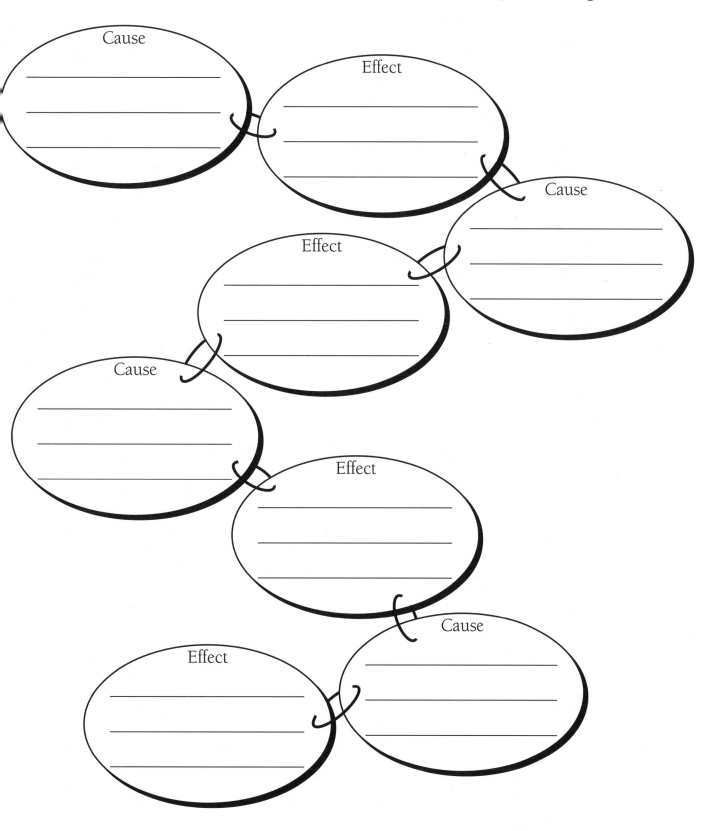

Standards-Based LANGUAGE ARTS
Graphic Organizers & Rubrics for Elementary Students

Cause-and-Effect Chain

Rubric

Rating Scale:

1	2	3
Completely	Some	Not Much

Directions to Student:

In the big loops of the chain, write the number that best tells how well you were able to understand and complete the cause-and-effect chain activity.

1. I was able to fill in each part of the CAUSE chain.

2. I was able to fill in each part of the EFFECT chain.

3. I was able to understand the relationship of CAUSE and EFFECT in each section of the chain.

4. I was able to figure out how each cause and effect section of the chain led to the ultimate or final EFFECT.

Comments by Student: _____

_____

_____

_____

Signed _____ Date _____

Comments by Teacher: _____

_____

_____

_____

Signed _____ Date _____

Standards-Based LANGUAGE ARTS
Graphic Organizers & Rubrics for Elementary Students

Copyright ©2004 by Incentive Publications, Inc.
Nashville, TN.

Chalk Talk Organizer

Topic _____

Time allotted for talk _____

_____

Format _____

_____

References _____

_____

Graphics _____

_____

Time line and steps for completion _____

_____

_____

Notes _____

_____

_____

_____

_____

_____

Standards-Based LANGUAGE ARTS
Graphic Organizers & Rubrics for Elementary Students

Chalk Talk Organizer

Rating Scale:

Needs Work	Acceptable	Very Good

1. REPORT FORMAT: My chalk talk is a brief oral presentation based on a storyboard with numbered frames, illustrations, and explanations of my topic.	
2. INFORMATION: The data in my chalk talk is well-researched, and the scope and sequence are presented in a logical order.	
3. GRAMMAR: My storyboard and chalk talk contain no grammar, spelling, or punctuation errors.	
4. INTEREST: My chalk talk and storyboard make my topic easier to understand and interesting to learn about.	
5. ORGANIZATION: My storyboard is constructed so that I can finish my oral delivery of content and the last details of the visual scenario at the same time.	
6. GRAPHICS/CREATIVITY: My chalk talk and storyboard use visuals and graphics creatively and effectively.	

Student/Teacher Conference Checklist

	Student	Teacher
1. Thorough Research		
2. Organization		
3. Attractive Presentation		
4. Audience Interest		
5. Creativity		
6. Met all requirements of project		
7. Evidence of effort		
8. Overall Rating		

Character Analysis Organizer

Graphic Organizer

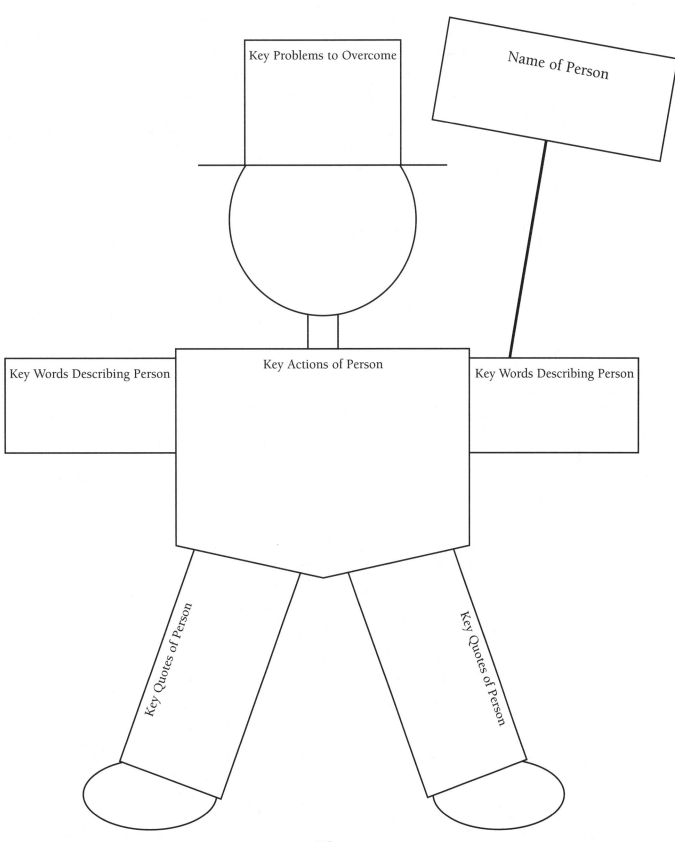

Key Problems to Overcome

Name of Person

Key Actions of Person

Key Words Describing Person

Key Words Describing Person

Key Quotes of Person

Key Quotes of Person

Standards-Based LANGUAGE ARTS
Graphic Organizers & Rubrics for Elementary Students

Character Analysis Organizer

Rubric

Rating Scale:

    0 = I did very little, if anything

    1 = I did some work, but not much

    2 = I did most of the work, although not all

    3 = I did everything I needed to, and more

1. I wrote the full name of the character.	Rating: _____
2. I wrote oodles of interesting words describing the character.	Rating: _____
3. I wrote lots of key actions of the character.	Rating: _____
4. I wrote many important deeds of the character.	Rating: _____
5. I wrote major problems the character had to overcome.	Rating: _____

Comments by Student: _____

_____

_____

_____

        Signed _____ Date _____

Comments by Teacher: _____

_____

_____

_____

        Signed _____ Date _____

Standards-Based LANGUAGE ARTS
Graphic Organizers & Rubrics for Elementary Students

Compare and Contrast Organizer

Graphic Organizer

Concept 1 _____

Concept 2 _____

HOW ALIKE?

_____
_____
_____
_____
_____

HOW DIFFERENT?

With Regard To

_____ ◀▶ _____
_____   _____
_____ ◀▶ _____
_____   _____
_____ ◀▶ _____

Compare and Contrast Organizer

Rubric

Rating Scale: ★ ★ ★   COMPETENT skills in making comparisons

★ ★ ☆   DEVELOPING skills in making comparisons

★ ☆ ☆   BEGINNING skills in making comparisons

Directions to Student:

Are you a three star (★★★), two star (★★) or one star (★) student on these tasks? Record your responses by shading in the right number of stars.

1. I learned how to research information about two different but related concepts.	☆ ☆ ☆
2. I learned how to record my ideas about ways these two concepts are alike.	☆ ☆ ☆
3. I learned how to record my ideas about ways these two concepts are different.	☆ ☆ ☆
4. I learned how to analyze the ways they are alike and different in regard to some specific criteria or characteristics.	☆ ☆ ☆
5. I learned the importance of being able to compare and contrast two different concepts.	☆ ☆ ☆

Comments by Student: _____

_____

_____

Signed _____ Date _____

Comments by Teacher: _____

_____

_____

Signed _____ Date _____

Standards-Based LANGUAGE ARTS
Graphic Organizers & Rubrics for Elementary Students

Concept Map

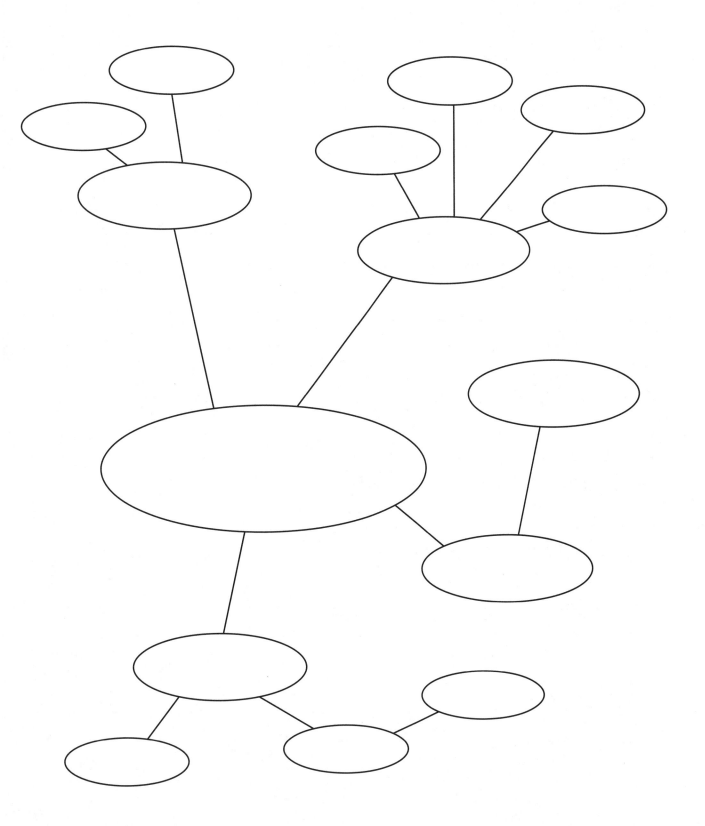

Standards-Based LANGUAGE ARTS
Graphic Organizers & Rubrics for Elementary Students

Concept Map

Rating Scale:

Bull's Eye    Good Shot    Miss

Directions to Student:

In the target at the end of each line, show how you rate your performance on this activity.

1. I can recognize a concept map.	
2. I can see a need for a concept map.	
3. I can describe a concept map.	
4. I can interpret a concept map.	
5. I can construct a concept map.	
6. I can teach someone else about concept maps.	

Comments by Student: _____

_____

_____

_____

Signed _____ Date _____

Comments by Teacher: _____

_____

_____

_____

Signed _____ Date _____

Crossword or Word Find Puzzle Grid

Graphic Organizer

Title_____

Standards-Based LANGUAGE ARTS
Graphic Organizers & Rubrics for Elementary Students

Crossword or Word Find Puzzle Grid

Rubric

Rating Scale:

Puzzle Wizard	Puzzle Apprentice	Puzzle Novice
★ ★ ★	★ ★ ☆	☆ ☆ ☆

Directions to Student:

Fill in the number of stars on each puzzle piece below that best describe how well you can design, construct, or complete either a crossword puzzle or a word find puzzle using the criteria listed below.

1. I can complete a word find puzzle that someone else has made.	☆ ☆ ☆
2. I can complete a crossword puzzle that someone else has made.	☆ ☆ ☆
3. I can create an original word find puzzle of my own.	☆ ☆ ☆
4. I can create an original crossword puzzle of my own.	☆ ☆ ☆
5. I can construct an interesting word find puzzle for others to do.	☆ ☆ ☆
6. I can construct an interesting crossword puzzle for others to do.	☆ ☆ ☆

Comments by Student: _____

_____

_____

_____

Signed _____ Date _____

Comments by Teacher: _____

_____

_____

_____

Signed _____ Date _____

Standards-Based LANGUAGE ARTS
Graphic Organizers & Rubrics for Elementary Students

Copyright ©2004 by Incentive Publications, Inc.
Nashville, TN.

Cube Report Organizer

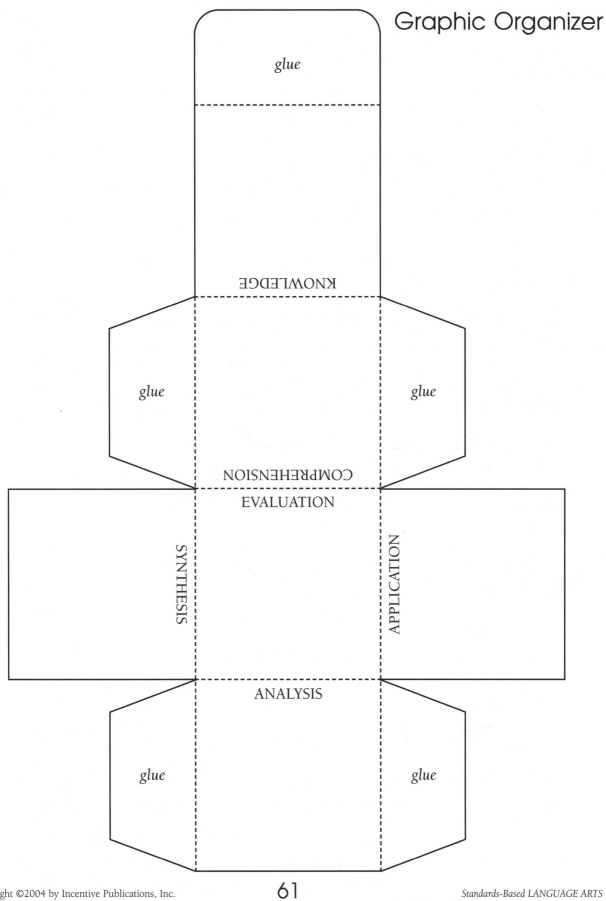

Standards-Based LANGUAGE ARTS
Graphic Organizers & Rubrics for Elementary Students

Cube Report Organizer

Rubric

Rating Scale:

1	2	3
Not Pleased with Myself	Somewhat Pleased with Myself	Very Pleased with Myself

Directions to Student:

For each of the sections of this six-sided cube, use the rating scale to rate your work for each level of Bloom's Taxonomy.

1. I researched my topic and reported information about it at the Knowledge level. ☐

2. I researched my topic and reported information about it at the Comprehension level. ☐

3. I researched my topic and reported information about it at the Application level. ☐

4. I researched my topic and reported information about it at the Analysis level. ☐

5. I researched my topic and reported information about it at the Synthesis level. ☐

6. I researched my topic and reported information about it at the Evaluation level. ☐

Comments by Student: _____

_____

_____

Signed _____ Date _____

Comments by Teacher: _____

_____

_____

Signed _____ Date _____

Cycle Organizer

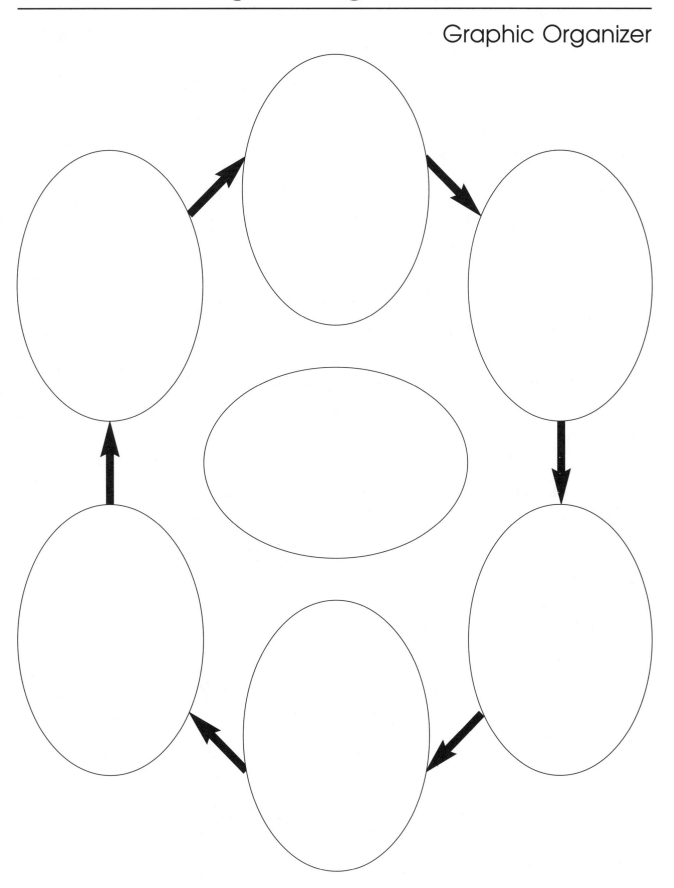

Standards-Based LANGUAGE ARTS
Graphic Organizers & Rubrics for Elementary Students

Cycle Organizer

Rating Scale: Sunshine   Cloudy   Rain

Directions to Student:

Use the criteria listed below to rate the quality of your Cycle Organizer. In the circle at the end of each question, draw and color the appropriate weather condition that describes how you feel about your work.

1. I understand the concept of "cycle."	
2. I was able to identify events that were important to the cycle.	
3. I was able to write down the events in their proper sequence.	
4. I was able to insert additional circles in the cycle as needed.	

Comments by Student: _____

_____

_____

_____

Signed _____ Date _____

Comments by Teacher: _____

_____

_____

_____

Signed _____ Date _____

Digging the Dictionary Study Guide

Directions to Student:

Column A: words beginning with specified blends are designated parts of speech.

Column B: words rearranged in ABC order.

Column C: good synonym for each word in Column B.

COLUMN A	COLUMN B	COLUMN C
cr — verb		
str — verb		
bl — adjective		
th — noun		
ea — adjective		
cl — adjective		
tr — verb		
fl — noun		
sn — noun		
dr — adjective		
on — adverb		
wr — verb		
ca — noun		
qu — adverb		
fa — verb		
ch — noun		
sp — noun		
gr — adjective		

Standards-Based LANGUAGE ARTS
Graphic Organizers & Rubrics for Elementary Students

Digging the Dictionary Study Guide

Rating Scale:　　　**A**　　　　　　　**B**　　　　　　　**C**
　　　　　　　　Excellent　　　　　　Good　　　　　　　Fair

Directions to Student:

In the box at the end of each line, rate the quality of your Digging the Dictionary organizer by writing the letter grade that best describes your performance.

1. I was able to use the dictionary to find words beginning with specified blends.	
2. I was able to rearrange the words in correct in alphabetical order.	
3. I was able to understand the parts of speech specified in COLUMN A.	
4. I was able to find a good synonym for each word in COLUMN B.	

Comments by Student: _____

_____

_____

_____

Signed _____ Date _____

Comments by Teacher: _____

_____

_____

_____

Signed _____ Date _____

5 Ws and How Web

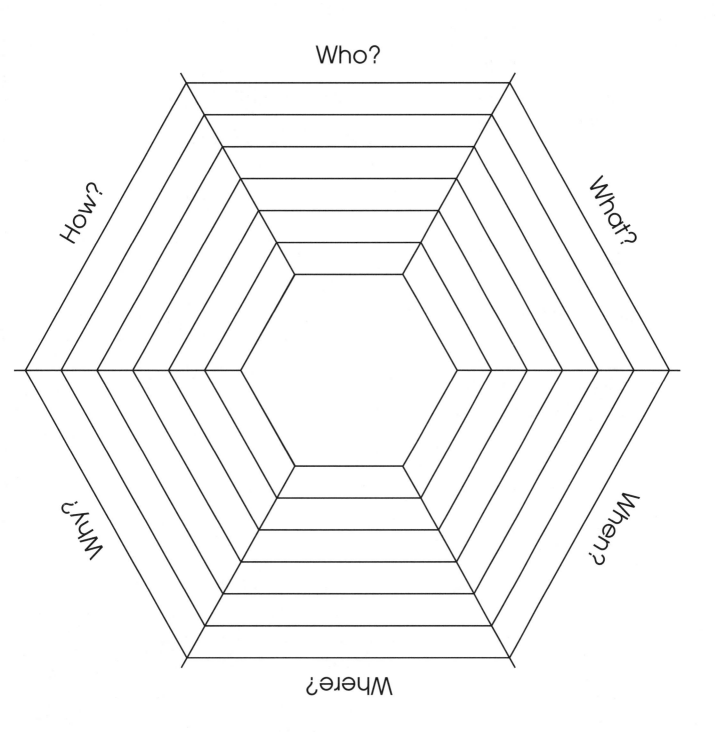

5 Ws and How Web

Rating Scale:

1	2	3
Star Reporter	Desk Reporter	Cub Reporter

Directions to Student:

In the box at the end of each line, write the number that best describes your work on this activity.

1. My "WHO" response is complete. ☐

2. My "WHAT" response is complete. ☐

3. My "WHEN" response is complete. ☐

4. My "WHERE" response is complete. ☐

5. My "WHY" response is complete. ☐

6. My "HOW" response is complete. ☐

7. My "SUMMARY" response is complete. ☐

Comments by Student: _____

_____

_____

_____

Signed _____ Date _____

Comments by Teacher: _____

_____

_____

_____

Signed _____ Date _____

Group Book Report Collage Plan

Graphic Organizer

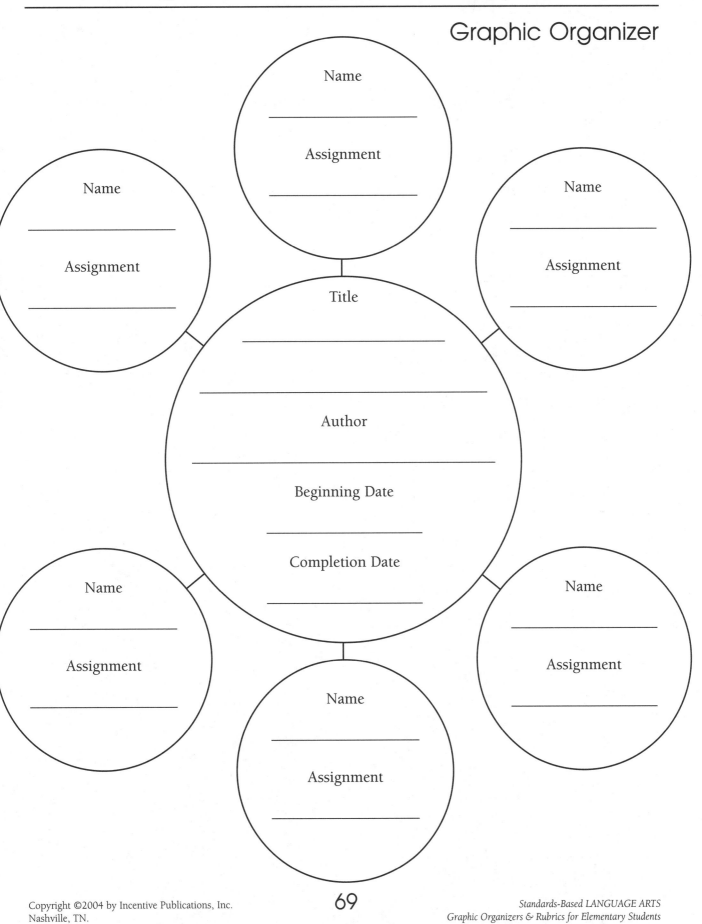

Name

_____

Assignment

_____

Name

_____

Assignment

_____

Name

_____

Assignment

_____

Title

_____

_____

Author

_____

Beginning Date

_____

Completion Date

_____

Name

_____

Assignment

_____

Name

_____

Assignment

_____

Name

_____

Assignment

_____

Standards-Based LANGUAGE ARTS
Graphic Organizers & Rubrics for Elementary Students

Group Book Report Collage Plan

Rubric

Rating Scale:

1	2	3
Maximum	Medium	Minimum

Directions to Student:

Before you begin your book report collage, list six different criteria to use in evaluating your finished product. Then rate the results of each one using the rating scale given here.

Criteria 1

Criteria 2

Criteria 3

Criteria 4

Criteria 5

Criteria 6

Standards-Based LANGUAGE ARTS
Graphic Organizers & Rubrics for Elementary Students

70

Copyright ©2004 by Incentive Publications, Inc.
Nashville, TN.

Group Report Mural Organizer

Name: _____

Topic: _____

Overall Theme of Mural: _____

Assigned Topic for Mural: _____

Ideas for My Mural Section: _____

_____

_____

Name

Assignment

Name

Assignment

Name

Assignment

Name

Assignment

Name

Assignment

Title or Topic

Author

Beginning Date   Completion Date

Name

Assignment

Standards-Based LANGUAGE ARTS
Graphic Organizers & Rubrics for Elementary Students

Group Report Mural Organizer

Directions to Student:

Place a check mark in the appropriate box.

	Excellent	Good	Fair	Poor
Group Interaction				
Individual Contributions				
Role Assignments				
Objectives				
Plan of Action				
Materials				
Use of Time				
Overall Rating				

Comments by Student: _____

_____

_____

_____

_____

_____

Signed _____ Date _____

Comments by Teacher: _____

_____

_____

_____

_____

_____

Signed _____ Date _____

Independent Study Planning Tool

Graphic Organizer

PERSONAL PROJECT PLAN

Title and Description of Study	Beginning Date	Format for Study
	_____	
	Completion Date	
	_____	

Resources Needed and Location

Challenges to be expected and/or questions to answer

Method of Evaluation

Standards-Based LANGUAGE ARTS
Graphic Organizers & Rubrics for Elementary Students

Independent Study Planning Tool

Rubric

Title of Project/Assignment: _____

Beginning Project Date: _____ Ending Project Date: _____

Rating Scale:

1	2	3	4
First Base	Second Base	Third Base	Home Run

Directions to Student:

In the box at the end of each line, write the number that best describes your performance on this activity.

1. I wrote down a title and detailed description of my study.	⬠
2. I developed a logical format for my study.	⬠
3. I noted expected challenges and answered key questions.	⬠
4. I succeeded in locating resources and evaluating study results.	⬠

Comments by Student: _____

_____

_____

_____

Signed _____ Date _____

Comments by Teacher: _____

_____

_____

_____

Signed _____ Date _____

Standards-Based LANGUAGE ARTS
Graphic Organizers & Rubrics for Elementary Students

Copyright ©2004 by Incentive Publications, Inc.
Nashville, TN.

Individual Project Plan Organizer

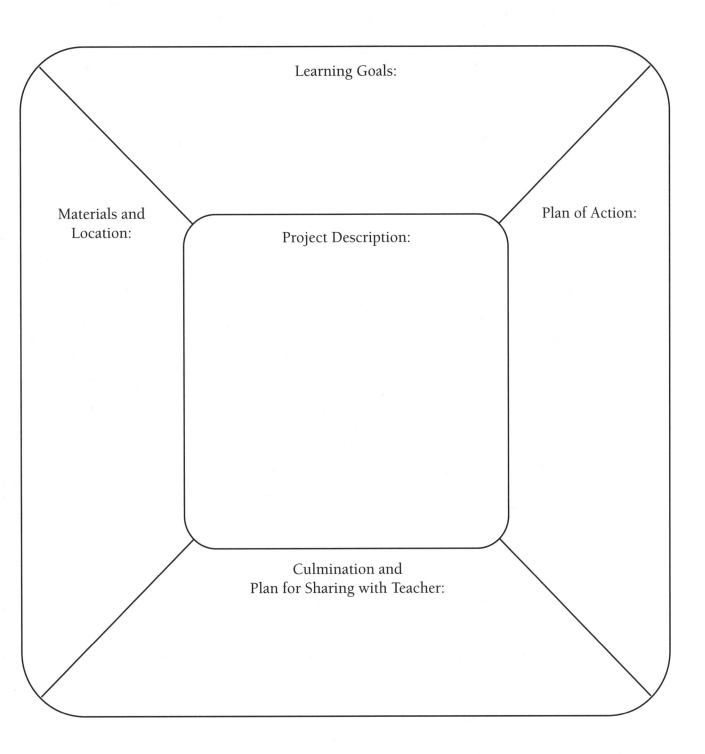

Learning Goals:

Materials and
Location:

Project Description:

Plan of Action:

Culmination and
Plan for Sharing with Teacher:

Individual Project Plan Organizer

Rubric

Rating Scale: Excellent   Good   Fair   Poor

                         1   2   3   4

Directions to Student:

In the box at the end of each line, write the number that best describes your performance on this activity.

1. **QUALITY OF MATERIALS AND LOCATION**
   I was able to make a list of the materials I needed for my project and where to find them.

2. **QUALITY OF LEARNING GOALS**
   I was able to write down at least three goals to guide my project from start to finish.

3. **QUALITY OF PLAN OF ACTION**
   I was able to outline the important steps, in sequence, for completing my project.

4. **QUALITY OF PLAN FOR SHARING WITH TEACHER**
   I was able to think of a good way to share the progress of my project with my teacher.

Comments by Student: _____

_____

_____

Signed _____ Date _____

Comments by Teacher: _____

_____

_____

Signed _____ Date _____

Standards-Based LANGUAGE ARTS
Graphic Organizers & Rubrics for Elementary Students

Interview Organizer

Getting Ready for the Interview

Name of Interviewee _____

Name of Interviewer _____

Date of Interview _____

Purpose of Interview _____

_____

Conducting the Interview

Question One _____

_____

Response _____

_____

Question Two _____

_____

Response _____

_____

Question Three _____

_____

Response _____

_____

Following the Interview

Results of the Interview _____

_____

_____

_____

Interview Organizer

Rating Scale: √+   √   √−

Very good   Acceptable   Needs work

Directions to Student:

At the end of each line, circle the appropriate rating for your performance.

1. I chose a special person as the interviewee.	√+	√	√−
2. I enjoyed my role as the interviewer.	√+	√	√−
3. I arranged a date for the interview.	√+	√	√−
4. I established a purpose for the interview.	√+	√	√−
5. I developed good questions for the interview.	√+	√	√−
6. I conducted the interview.	√+	√	√−
7. I did follow-up work after the interview.	√+	√	√−
8. I summarized the results of the interview.	√+	√	√−

Student/Teacher Conference Checklist

	Student	Teacher
1. Appropriate interviewee selection		
2. Evidence of effort on part of interviewer		
3. Quality of interview questions		
4. Organization of interview process		
5. Creative follow-up after interview		
6. Met all requirements of interview project		

Journalist's Template

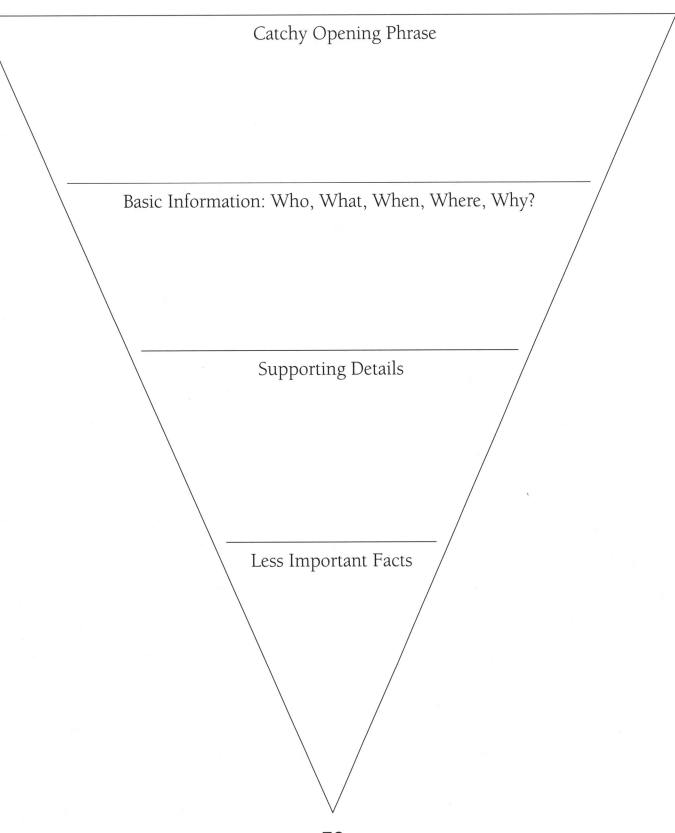

Catchy Opening Phrase

Basic Information: Who, What, When, Where, Why?

Supporting Details

Less Important Facts

Journalist's Template

Rubric

Rating Scale:

Slow Down | Keep Going | Right On | WOW

Directions to Student:

In the box at the end of each line, write the phrase that best describes your work on this activity.

1. Quality of my catchy opening phrase.

2. Quality of my basic information:
   Who, What, When, Where, and Why?

3. Quality of my supporting details.

4. Quality of my less important facts.

Comments by Student: _____

_____

_____

_____

Signed _____ Date _____

Comments by Teacher: _____

_____

_____

_____

Signed _____ Date _____

Standards-Based LANGUAGE ARTS
Graphic Organizers & Rubrics for Elementary Students

Literature Analysis Stairway

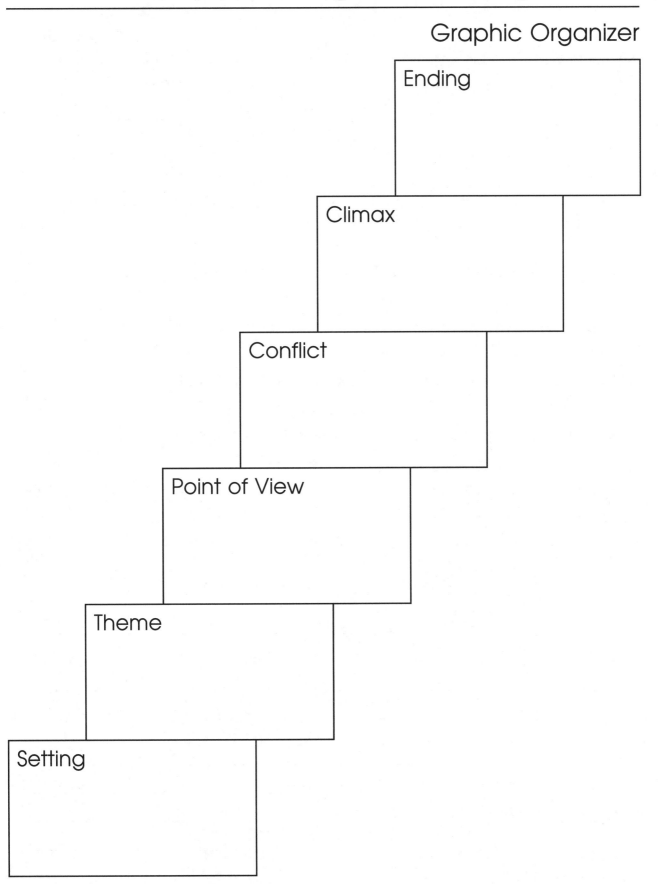

Ending

Climax

Conflict

Point of View

Theme

Setting

Standards-Based LANGUAGE ARTS
Graphic Organizers & Rubrics for Elementary Students

Literature Analysis Stairway

Rating Scale:
At the Top
of the Stairs

Halfway Up
the Stairs

At the Bottom
of the Stairs

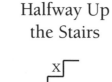

Directions to Student:

In the box at the end of each line, write an "x" to show the level of your performance on this activity.

1. I know how to identify the climax of a short story, novel, or poem.

2. I know how to describe the setting of a short story, novel, or poem.

3. I know how to explain the theme of a short story, novel, or poem.

4. I know how to summarize the conflict in a short story, novel, or poem.

5. I know how to determine the point of view in a short story, novel, or poem.

6. I know how to discuss the ending of the story with another person.

Comments by Student: _____

_____

_____

_____

Signed _____ Date _____

Comments by Teacher: _____

_____

_____

_____

Signed _____ Date _____

Multiple Tasks Planning Guide

Graphic Organizer

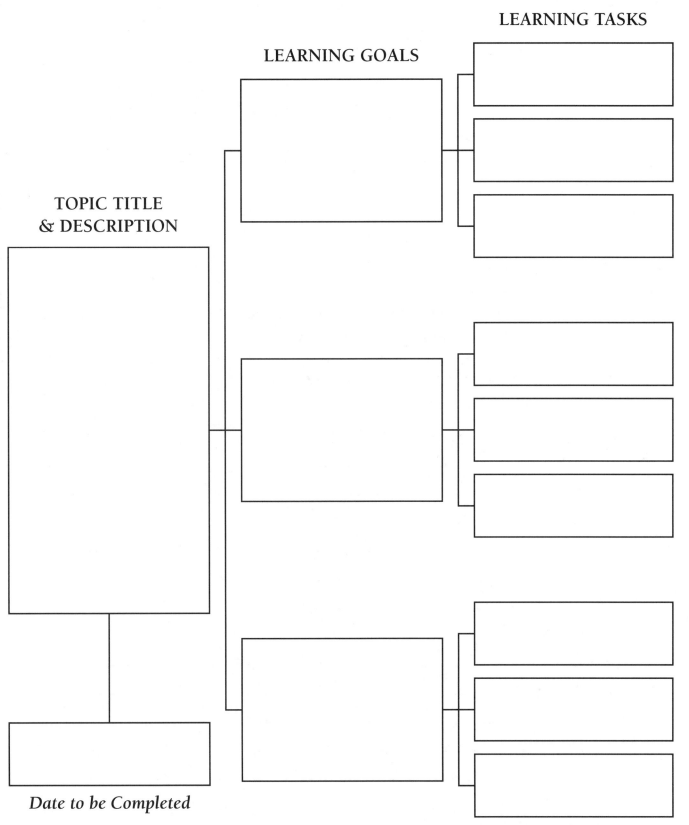

LEARNING TASKS

LEARNING GOALS

TOPIC TITLE & DESCRIPTION

Date to be Completed

Standards-Based LANGUAGE ARTS
Graphic Organizers & Rubrics for Elementary Students

Multiple Tasks Planning Guide

Rubric

Rating Scale: Excellent   Good   Poor
                              3   2   1

Directions to Student:

In the box at the end of each line, write the number that best describes your work on this activity.

1. I was able to find an appropriate topic title and description for this activity.	
2. I was able to plan a date for this activity to be completed.	
3. I was able to find the learning goals associated with the topic title and description for this activity.	
4. I was able to outline the necessary learning tasks for this activity.	

Comments by Student: _____

_____

_____

_____

_____

Signed _____ Date _____

Comments by Teacher: _____

_____

_____

_____

_____

Signed _____ Date _____

Standards-Based LANGUAGE ARTS
Graphic Organizers & Rubrics for Elementary Students

Observation Log

Date: _____ Time: _____

Observation: _____

_____

_____

_____

_____

_____

_____

_____

_____

_____

Date: _____ Time: _____

Observation: _____

_____

_____

_____

_____

_____

_____

_____

_____

_____

Standards-Based LANGUAGE ARTS
Graphic Organizers & Rubrics for Elementary Students

Observation Log

Rubric

Rating Scale:

  Eyes wide open

 Eyes half shut

  Eyes shut

Directions to Student:

At the end of each question, write the phrase that best describes your own results on this activity.

1. I understand the purpose of an observation log.	
2. I understand how to record my observations of an event or action over time.	
3. I understand how to describe the changes I see in my observations of an event or action over time.	
4. I understand how to interpret the findings of my observations of an event or action over time.	
5. I understand how to summarize the results of my observations of an event or action over time.	

Comments by Student: _____

_____

_____

Signed _____ Date _____

Comments by Teacher: _____

_____

_____

Signed _____ Date _____

Standards-Based LANGUAGE ARTS
Graphic Organizers & Rubrics for Elementary Students

Portfolio Planning Guide

Graphic Organizer

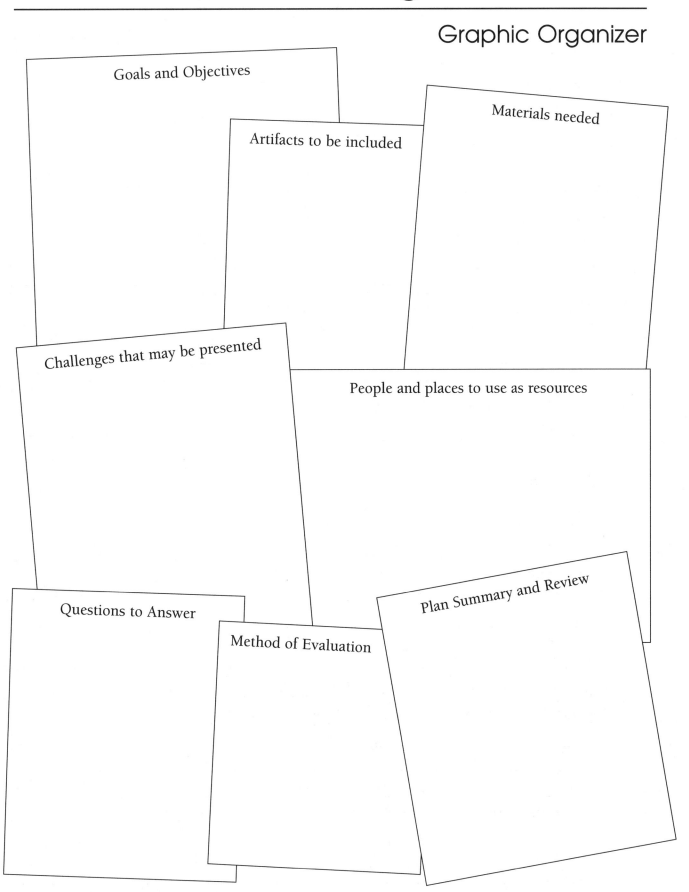

Goals and Objectives

Artifacts to be included

Materials needed

Challenges that may be presented

People and places to use as resources

Questions to Answer

Method of Evaluation

Plan Summary and Review

Standards-Based LANGUAGE ARTS
Graphic Organizers & Rubrics for Elementary Students

Portfolio Planning Guide

Directions to Student:

Use the following questions to help you review and reflect on how you completed your project or portfolio.

1. Was my project or portfolio based on meaningful goals, and well planned to carry out the goals?

   _____

   _____

2. What do I know now that I did not know before?

   _____

   _____

3. What are strengths of my work?

   _____

   _____

4. What could I have done better?

   _____

   _____

5. Does my work show a creative approach?

   _____

   _____

6. Using A for excellent, B for good, C for acceptable, and D for barely or not acceptable, what letter grade would I give myself, and why?

   _____

   _____

7. What would I do differently if I were doing this project again?

   _____

   _____

Prediction Web

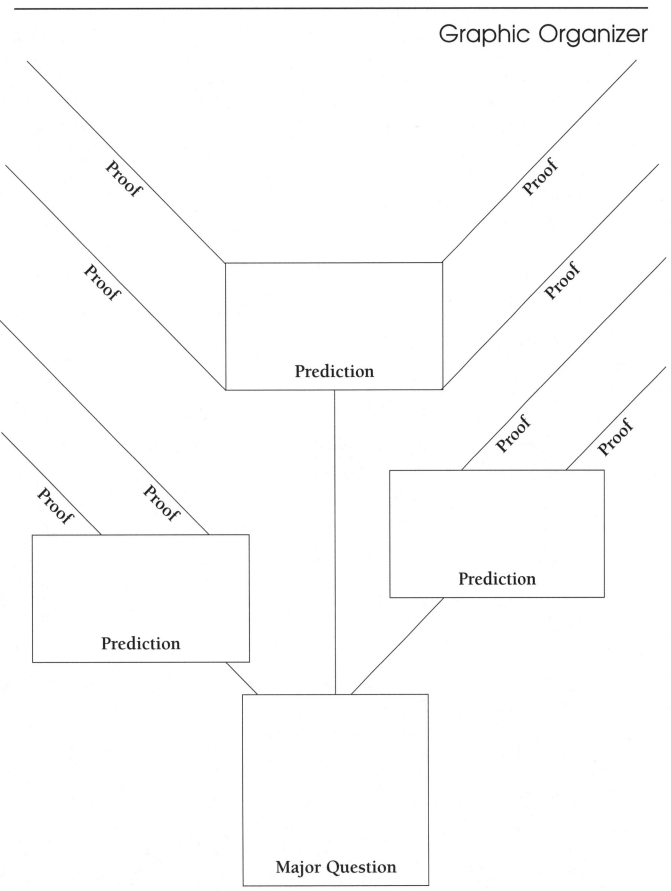

Proof

Proof

Proof

Proof

Proof

Proof

Proof

Proof

Prediction

Prediction

Prediction

Major Question

Standards-Based LANGUAGE ARTS
Graphic Organizers & Rubrics for Elementary Students

Prediction Web

Rubric

Rating Scale: Best of Show   Good Show   Fair Show   Poor Show

1   2   3   4

Directions to Student:

In the box at the end of each line, write the number that best describes your work on this activity.

1. I know the purpose of a prediction web.

2. I know how to choose a major topic or problem for use with a prediction web.

3. I know how to brainstorm possible predictions or probable outcomes in response to the major topic or problem of a prediction web.

4. I know how to record proof to support or negate the predictions on a prediction web.

5. I know there are many different applications for using a prediction web.

Comments by Student: _____

_____

_____

Signed _____ Date _____

Comments by Teacher: _____

_____

_____

Signed _____ Date _____

Problem-Solving Star

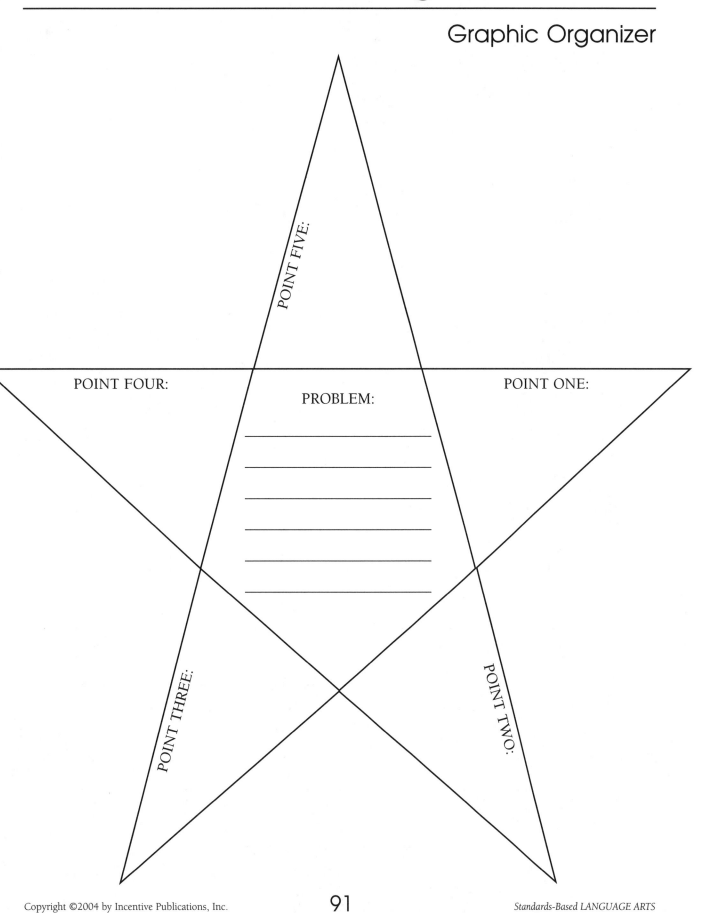

POINT FIVE:

POINT FOUR:

POINT ONE:

PROBLEM:

_____

_____

_____

_____

_____

_____

POINT THREE:

POINT TWO:

Standards-Based LANGUAGE ARTS
Graphic Organizers & Rubrics for Elementary Students

Problem-Solving Star

Rating Scale: ★ ★ ★ Shooting Star
                   ★ ★ ☆ Falling Star
                   ★ ☆ ☆ Star Struck

Directions to Student:

Shade the appropriate number of stars for your performance on this activity.

1. I enjoy problem solving.	☆ ☆ ☆
2. I wrote a good problem to solve in the center of the star.	☆ ☆ ☆
3. I thought of several key points or solutions to the problem and placed them at the points of the star.	☆ ☆ ☆
4. I researched information to help me solve this problem.	☆ ☆ ☆
5. I would know how to do another problem-solving star by myself next time I had a problem to solve.	☆ ☆ ☆

Comments by Student: _____

_____

_____

_____

_____

Signed _____ Date _____

Comments by Teacher: _____

_____

_____

_____

Signed _____ Date _____

Scope and Sequence Chart

Historical Setting
Historical Figures
Historical Problem Situation
First Event/Step:
Second Event/Step:
Third Event/Step:
Fourth Event/Step:
Fifth Event/Step:
Outcome(s)
Resolution

Scope and Sequence Chart

Rubric

Rating Scale:

1	2	3
Yes	Kind Of	Not Really

Directions to Student:

In the box at the end of the line, write the number that best describes your work on this activity.

1. Quality of my first date, event, or step of task.	☐
2. Quality of my second date, event, or step of task.	☐
3. Quality of my third date, event, or step of task.	☐
4. Quality of my fourth date, event, or step of task.	☐
5. Quality of my fifth date, event, or step of task.	☐
6. Quality of my additional dates, events, or steps of task.	☐
7. Quality of my overall chart.	☐

Comments by Student: _____

_____

_____

_____

_____

Signed _____ Date _____

Comments by Teacher: _____

_____

_____

_____

_____

Signed _____ Date _____

Standards-Based LANGUAGE ARTS
Graphic Organizers & Rubrics for Elementary Students

Copyright ©2004 by INCENTIVE PUBLICATIONS, Inc.
Nashville, TN.

SQ3R Chart

Directions to Student:

Use **one** chart for each major section of the chapter. Remember that SQ3R means:

Survey: Read titles/subtitles. Notice words/phrases in special type. Skim illustrations/
            charts/graphs. Review end-of-chapter summaries and questions.

Question: Turn main/subtopics in special print into 5W questions—Who, What, When,
            Where, and Why.

Read: Read information to answer questions, highlight main ideas, and make notes.

Recite: Pause at the end of each chapter section to answer questions orally,
            using your own words.

Review: Construct a study guide sheet with summaries and main ideas from
            your reading.

Survey: Record most important titles and subtitles from major chapter section.

_____

_____

_____

_____

_____

Question: Write Who, What, When, Where, and Why questions for main/subtopics.

_____

_____

_____

_____

_____

Read: Write short answers to five questions from above.

_____

_____

_____

_____

_____

Standards-Based LANGUAGE ARTS
Graphic Organizers & Rubrics for Elementary Students

SQ3R Chart

Rubric

Rating Scale: 2   1   0
Very Good   Needs Improvement   Does Not Meet Criteria

Directions to Student/Teacher:

In the box at the end of each question, write the number that best measures performance.

Task	Student Rating	Teacher Rating
1. Ability to SURVEY (Read titles/subtitles, notice words/ phrases, skim illustrations/charts/graphs, and review end-of-chapter summaries/questions)		
2. Ability to QUESTION (Turn main ideas in special print into 5W questions of Who, What, When, Where, and Why)		
3. Ability to READ (Read information to answer questions, highlight main ideas, and take notes)		
4. Ability to RECITE (Pause at end of chapter section to answer questions orally, using my own words)		
5. Ability to REVIEW (Construct a study guide sheet with summaries and main ideas from my reading)		

Comments by Student: _____

_____

_____

Signed _____ Date _____

Comments by Teacher: _____

_____

_____

Signed _____ Date _____

Standards-Based LANGUAGE ARTS
Graphic Organizers & Rubrics for Elementary Students

Storyboard Organizer

1.

6.

2.

7.

3.

8.

4.

9.

5.

10.

Standards-Based LANGUAGE ARTS
Graphic Organizers & Rubrics for Elementary Students

Storyboard Organizer

Rating Scale: Not Successful   Very Successful

1   2   3   4   5

Directions to Student:

In the box at the end of each line, write the number that best describes your work on this activity.

1. Quality of Storyboard Format	☐
2. Quality of Information Presented	☐
3. Quality of Details and/or Descriptions	☐
4. Quality of Grammar	☐
5. Quality of Interest	☐
6. Quality of Creative Thinking	☐

Comments by Student: _____

_____

_____

_____

Signed _____ Date _____

Comments by Teacher: _____

_____

_____

_____

Signed _____ Date _____

Surfing the Net Organizer

Graphic Organizer

Directions to Student:

Use the Internet to locate a website where you can find information about each of the different genres in literature that would appeal to kids your age. Record your website in each of the special circles below.

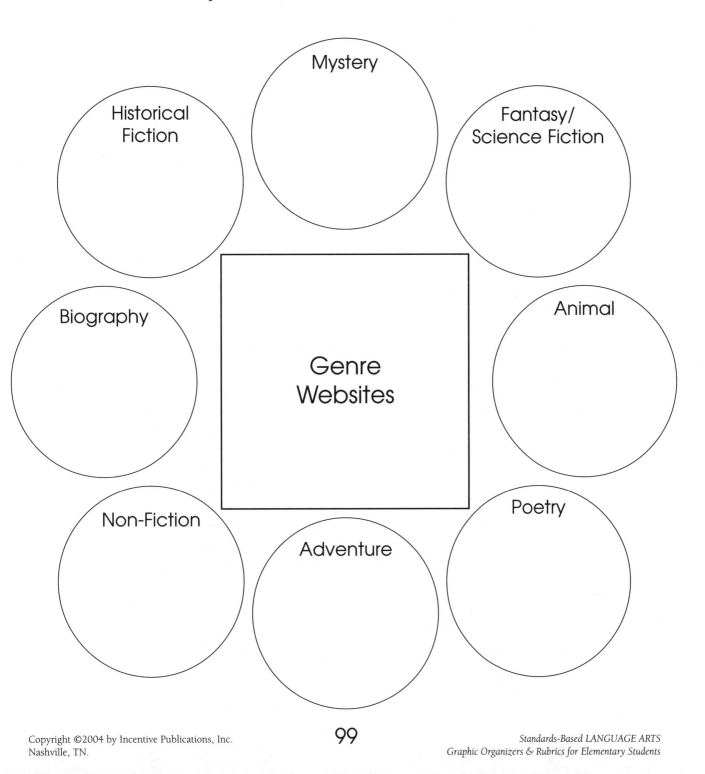

Standards-Based LANGUAGE ARTS
Graphic Organizers & Rubrics for Elementary Students

Surfing the Net Organizer

Rubric

Rating Scale: 1 2 3
GOOD   OK   NOT SO GOOD

Directions to Student:

In the box at the end of each line, write the number that best describes your work on this activity.

1. I was able to find a website for the poetry genre.	☐
2. I was able to find a website for the adventure genre.	☐
3. I was able to find a website for the fantasy/science fiction genre.	☐
4. I was able to find a website for the animal genre.	☐
5. I was able to find a website for the biography genre.	☐
6. I was able to find a website for the mystery genre.	☐
7. I was able to find a website for the non-fiction genre.	☐
8. I was able to find a website for the historical fiction genre.	☐

Comments by Student: _____

_____

_____

_____

Signed _____ Date _____

Comments by Teacher: _____

_____

_____

_____

Signed _____ Date _____

Standards-Based LANGUAGE ARTS
Graphic Organizers & Rubrics for Elementary Students

Tall Tale Organizer

Graphic Organizer

A . . .   N . . .

B . . .   O . . .

C . . .   P . . .

D . . .   Q . . .

E . . .   R . . .

F . . .   S . . .

G . . .   T . . .

H . . .   U . . .

I . . .   V . . .

J . . .   W . . .

K . . .   X . . .

L . . .   Y . . .

M . . .   Z . . .

Standards-Based LANGUAGE ARTS
Graphic Organizers & Rubrics for Elementary Students

Tall Tale Organizer

Rating Scale:

A	B	C
Amazing	Better Than Last Time	Careless Mistakes

Directions to Student:

In the box at the end of each line, write the letter that best describes your performance on this activity.

1. I was able to use most of the letters of the alphabet in my story/report.	
2. I was able to think of a good sentence for each letter used in my story/report.	
3. I was able to make the lines of my story/report interesting to the reader.	
4. I was able to arrange my thoughts so they made sense when the story/report was read.	
5. I was able to break up my story into at least three paragraphs.	
6. I was able to use some new and unusual words in the writing of my story/report ideas.	

Comments by Student: _____

_____

_____

Signed _____ Date _____

Comments by Teacher: _____

_____

_____

Signed _____ Date _____

Topic Tree Organizer

Standards-Based LANGUAGE ARTS
Graphic Organizers & Rubrics for Elementary Students

Topic Tree Organizer

Rating Scale:

Bull's Eye    Good Shot    Miss

Directions to Student:

In the target at the end of each line, fill in the number of circles that best show your work on this activity.

1. I can tell you how and when to use a Topic Tree.	
2. I can write a major topic in the oval at the top of the Topic Tree.	
3. I can write sub-headings on a major topic in the smaller ovals on the Topic Tree.	
4. I can write facts and information on the diagonal lines that extend from the sub-headings on the Topic Tree.	
5. I can use a Topic Tree to structure my ideas on a topic in any content area.	

Comments by Student: _____

_____

_____

Signed _____ Date _____

Comments by Teacher: _____

_____

_____

Signed _____ Date _____

Umbrella Organizer

Standards-Based LANGUAGE ARTS
Graphic Organizers & Rubrics for Elementary Students

Umbrella Organizer

Rubric

Rating Scale:

1	2	3
Heavy Thunderstorms	Rain Predicted	Rainbow Sighted

Directions to Student:

Circle the umbrella that describes your work on this activity.

1. I was able to summarize the main idea or concept and write it on the inside of the umbrella outline in two or three sentences.

2. I was able to write down at least five major details or related ideas on the lines located to the right of the umbrella.

3. I was able to write down at least five minor details or related ideas on the lines located to the left of the umbrella.

4. I was able to think of more than five minor or major details/related ideas for the lines next to the umbrella.

Comments by Student: _____

_____

_____

Signed _____ Date _____

Comments by Teacher: _____

_____

_____

Signed _____ Date _____

Standards-Based LANGUAGE ARTS
Graphic Organizers & Rubrics for Elementary Students

Copyright ©2004 by Incentive Publications, Inc.
Nashville, TN.

Vocabulary Learning Ladder

Graphic Organizer

Word or Term: _____

Textbook Sentence: _____

Page: _____ Definition: _____

_____

5

Word or Term: _____

Textbook Sentence: _____

Page: _____ Definition: _____

_____

4

Word or Term: _____

Textbook Sentence: _____

Page: _____ Definition: _____

_____

3

Word or Term: _____

Textbook Sentence: _____

Page: _____ Definition: _____

_____

2

Word or Term: _____

Textbook Sentence: _____

Page: _____ Definition: _____

_____

1

Standards-Based LANGUAGE ARTS
Graphic Organizers & Rubrics for Elementary Students

Vocabulary Learning Ladder

Rubric

Rating Scale: 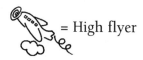 = High flyer   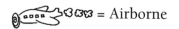 = Airborne   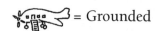 = Grounded

1. Have I learned how the Vocabulary Learning Ladder is useful in helping me expand my understanding of new words?

2. Have I written in a new word on each step of the ladder?

3. Have I recorded the appropriate sentence from the textbook for each new word?

4. Have I noted the page in the textbook where each new word and sentence may be found?

5. Have I defined each new word for future reference?

Comments by Student: _____

_____

_____

_____

Signed _____ Date _____

Comments by Teacher: _____

_____

_____

_____

Signed _____ Date _____

Standards-Based LANGUAGE ARTS
Graphic Organizers & Rubrics for Elementary Students

Copyright ©2004 by Incentive Publications, Inc.
Nashville, TN.

What, So What, Now What? Chart

Graphic Organizer

Topic of Study/Title _____

Student's Name _____

What?	So What?	Now What?

Standards-Based LANGUAGE ARTS
Graphic Organizers & Rubrics for Elementary Students

What, So What, Now What? Chart

Rubric

Rating Scale: ■■■ Very Good   ■■□ Good   ■□□ Not So Good

Directions to Student:

Shade in the number of blocks to show your rating.

1. I have been able to apply this "WHAT" pattern to my work. □ □ □

2. I have been able to record a response to the question:
   "WHAT" is the meaning of this piece
   and/or what did I learn from it? □ □ □

3. I have been able to record a series of responses to the question:
   "SO WHAT" difference does it make now that I know this,
   or what is its importance? □ □ □

4. I have been able to record an answer to the question:
   "NOW WHAT" can I do to use this information so that
   it makes a difference in what I know or can do or
   so I understand how it is important and relates to
   the major theme of study? □ □ □

Comments by Student: _____

_____

_____

Signed _____ Date _____

Comments by Teacher: _____

_____

_____

Signed _____ Date _____

Standards-Based LANGUAGE ARTS
Graphic Organizers & Rubrics for Elementary Students

Appendix

International Reading Association/
National Council of Teachers of English
English/Language Arts Standards
Grades K-8

Standard 1:

Students read a wide range of print and nonprint text to build an understanding of texts, of themselves, and of the cultures of the United States and the world, to acquire new information, to respond to the needs and demands of society and the workplace, and for personal fulfillment. Among these texts are fiction and nonfiction, classic and contemporary works.

Standard 2:

Students read a wide range of literature from many periods in many genres to build an understanding of the many dimensions (e.g., philosophical, ethical, aesthetic) of human experience.

Standard 3:

Students apply a wide range of strategies to comprehend, interpret, evaluate, and appreciate texts. They draw on their prior experience, their interactions with other readers and writers, their knowledge of word meaning and of other texts, their identification strategies, and their understanding of textual features (e.g., sound-letter correspondence, sentence structure, context, graphics).

Standard 4:

Students adjust their use of spoken, written, and visual language (e.g., conventions, style, vocabulary) to communicate effectively with a variety of audiences for a variety of purposes.

Standard 5:

Students employ a wide range of strategies as they write and use different writing process elements appropriately to communicate with different audiences for a variety of purposes.

Standards for the English Language Arts, by the International Reading Association and the National Council of Teachers of English, Copyright 1996 by the International Reading Association and the National Council of Teacher of English. Reprinted with permission.

Standard 6:

Students apply knowledge of language structure, language conventions (e.g., spelling and punctuation), media techniques, figurative language, and genre to create, critique, and discuss print and non-print texts.

Standard 7:

Students conduct research on issues and interests by generating ideas and questions, and by posing problems. They gather, evaluate, and synthesize data from a variety of sources (e.g., print and non-print texts, artifacts, people) to communicate their discoveries in ways that suit their purpose and audience.

Standard 8:

Students use a variety of technological and informational resources (e.g., libraries, databases, computer networks, video) to gather and synthesize information and to create and to communicate knowledge.

Standard 9:

Students develop an understanding of and respect for diversity in language use, patterns, and dialects across cultures, ethnic groups, geographic regions, and social roles.

Standard 10:

Students whose first language is not English make use of their first language to develop competency in the English language arts and to develop understanding of content across the curriculum.

Standard 11:

Students participate as knowledgeable, reflective, creative, and critical members of a variety of literacy communities.

Standard 12:

Students use spoken, written, and visual language to accomplish their own purposes (e.g., for learning, enjoyment, persuasion, and the exchange of information).

Planning Matrix

Correlatives: National Language Arts Standards as identified by the National Council of Teachers of English and the International Reading Association with activities and projects in Standards-Based Language Arts Graphic Organizers & Rubrics for Elementary Students, Incentive Publications, 2004.

Standards	Graphic Organizers	Rubrics
STANDARD 1: Students read a wide range of print and nonprint text to build an understanding of texts, of themselves, and of the cultures of the United States and the world, to acquire new information, to respond to the needs and demands of society and the workplace, and for personal fulfillment. Among these texts are fiction and nonfiction, classic and contemporary works.	31, 37, 39, 45, 61, 65, 67, 73, 79, 81, 85, 97, 109	32, 38, 40, 46, 62, 66, 68, 74, 80, 82, 86, 98, 110
STANDARD 2: Students read a wide range of literature from many periods in many genres to build an understanding of the many dimensions (e.g., philosophical, ethical, aesthetic) of human experience.	33, 45, 61, 63, 77, 79, 81, 85, 89, 99	34, 46, 62, 64, 78, 80, 82, 86, 90, 100
STANDARD 3: Students apply a wide range of strategies to comprehend, interpret, evaluate, and appreciate texts. They draw on their prior experience, their interactions with other readers and writers, their knowledge of word meaning and of other texts, their identification strategies, and their understanding of textual features (e.g., sound-letter correspondence, sentence structure, context, graphics).	41, 47, 57, 59, 61, 65, 67, 75, 87, 95, 97, 103, 105, 107	42, 48, 58, 60, 62, 66, 68, 76, 88, 96, 98, 104, 106, 108
STANDARD 4: Students adjust their use of spoken, written, and visual language (e.g., conventions, style, vocabulary) to communicate effectively with a variety of audiences for a variety of purposes.	39, 49, 53, 55, 63, 69, 71, 73, 77, 83, 85, 97	40, 50, 54, 56, 64, 72, 74, 84, 86, 98

Standards for the English Language Arts, by the International Reading Association and the National Council of Teachers of English,

Standards-Based LANGUAGE ARTS Graphic Organizers & Rubrics for Elementary Students

Planning Matrix

Correlatives: National Language Arts Standards as identified by the National Council of Teachers of English and the International Reading Association with activities and projects in

Standards-Based Language Arts Graphic Organizers & Rubrics for Elementary Students, Incentive Publications, 2004.

Standards	Graphic Organizers	Rubrics
STANDARD 5: Students employ a wide range of strategies as they write and use different writing process elements appropriately to communicate with different audiences for a variety of purposes.	51, 57, 61, 65, 69, 71, 73, 79, 89, 101, 107	52, 58, 62, 66, 70, 72, 74, 80, 90, 102, 108
STANDARD 6: Students apply knowledge of language structure, language conventions (e.g., spelling and punctuation), media techniques, figurative language, and genre to create, critique, and discuss print and non-print texts.	41, 65, 79, 81, 89, 93, 101, 103, 107, 109	42, 66, 80, 82, 90, 94, 102, 104, 108, 110
STANDARD 7: Students conduct research on issues and interests by generating ideas and questions, and by posing problems. They gather, evaluate, and synthesize data from a variety of sources (e.g., print and non-print texts, artifacts, people) to communicate their discoveries in ways that suit their purpose and audience.	35, 41, 43, 51, 67, 71, 73, 77, 85, 87, 89, 91, 103, 109	36, 42, 44, 52, 64, 68, 72, 74, 78, 86, 88, 90, 92, 104, 110
STANDARD 8: Students use a variety of technological and informational resources (e.g., libraries, databases, computer networks, video) to gather and synthesize information and to create and to communicate knowledge.	47, 51, 61, 65, 73, 79, 87, 93, 99	48, 52, 62, 66, 74, 80, 88, 94, 100

Standards for the English Language Arts, by the International Reading Association and the National Council of Teachers of English, Copyright 1996 by the International Reading Association and the National Council of Teacher of English. Reprinted with permission.

Standards-Based LANGUAGE ARTS
Graphic Organizers & Rubrics for Elementary Students

Planning Matrix

Correlatives: National Language Arts Standards as identified by the National Council of Teachers of English and the International Reading Association with activities and projects in Standards-Based Language Arts Graphic Organizers & Rubrics for Elementary Students, Incentive Publications, 2004.

Standards	Graphic Organizers	Rubrics
STANDARD 9: Students develop an understanding of and respect for diversity in language use, patterns, and dialects across cultures, ethnic groups, geographic regions, and social roles.	55, 59, 63, 77, 85, 87, 93, 101	56, 60, 64, 78, 86, 88, 94, 102
STANDARD 10: Students whose first language is not English make use of their first language to develop competency in the English language arts and to develop understanding of content across the curriculum.	47, 65, 67, 79, 83, 97, 101, 107	48, 66, 68, 80, 84, 98, 102, 108
STANDARD 11: Students participate as knowledgeable, reflective, creative, and critical members of a variety of literacy communities.	45, 49, 53, 63, 67, 85, 105, 109	46, 50, 54, 64, 68, 86, 106, 110
STANDARD 12: Students use spoken, written, and visual language to accomplish their own purposes (e.g., for learning, enjoyment, persuasion, and the exchange of information).	51, 53, 57, 59, 61, 69, 71, 73, 75, 83, 87, 89, 97, 101, 109	52, 54, 58, 60, 62, 70, 72, 74, 76, 84, 88, 90, 98, 102, 110

Standards for the English Language Arts, by the International Reading Association and the National Council of Teachers of English,

GUIDELINES
for Using Graphic Organizers

1. Graphic organizers can be used for curriculum planning, helping students process information, and as pre- or post-assessment tasks. Determine which types of graphic organizers are best for each purpose.

2. Graphic organizers are a performance-based model of assessment and make excellent artifacts for inclusion in a student portfolio. Decide which concepts in your discipline are best represented by the use of these organizers.

3. Use graphic organizers to help students focus on important concepts while omitting extraneous details.

4. Use graphic organizers as visual pictures to help the student remember key ideas.

5. Use graphic organizers to connect visual language with verbal language in active learning settings.

6. Use graphic organizers to enhance recall of important information.

7. Use graphic organizers to provide student motivation and relieve student boredom.

8. Use graphic organizers to show and explain relationships between and among varied content areas.

9. Use graphic organizers to make traditional lesson plans more interactive and more appealing to the visual learner.

10. Use graphic organizers to break down complex ideas through concise and structured visuals.

11. Use graphic organizers to help students note patterns and clarify ideas.

12. Use graphic organizers to help students better understand the concept of "part to whole."

13. Emphasize the use of graphic organizers to stimulate creative thinking.

14. Make sure there is a match between the type of organizer and the content being taught.

15. Make sure that using a graphic organizer is the best use of time when teaching a concept.

16. Use a wide variety of graphic organizers and use them collaboratively whenever possible.

GUIDELINES
for Using Rubrics

1. The rubric reflects the most important elements of an assigned task, product, or performance and enables both student and teacher to depict accurately the level of competence or stage of development of individual students.

2. The rubric is planned to augment, reinforce, personalize, and strengthen (but not replace) the assessment program mandated by curriculum guidelines or system requirements.

3. The rubric encourages student self-evaluation and can be shared with students prior to beginning the task so that students know exactly what represents quality work.

4. The rubric has two components which are: (1) characteristics or criteria for quality work on a specific task, and (2) determination of the specific levels of proficiency or degrees of success for each part of a task.

5. The rubric is designed to explain more concretely what a child knows and can do and is less subjective and more focused than other means of student evaluation.

6. Rating scales have been created to evaluate student performance. Easy-to-use weights for each answer make the results clear and specific.

7. If the rubric is holistic, it consists of paragraphs arranged in a hierarchy so that each level of proficiency has a paragraph describing factors that would result in that specific level.

8. If the rubric is analytical, it consists of a listing of criteria most characteristic of that task accompanied with the degrees of success for each model listed separately beside or under each criterion.

9. Samples of student work have been studied to determine realistic attributes common to varied performances at different levels of proficiency. These attributes have been translated into descriptors for the degrees of proficiency and to establish a rating scale to delineate those degrees of proficiency.

10. The rubric is accompanied by carefully planned opportunities for meta-cognitive reflections to provide for self-assessment observations completely unique to the students' own learning goals, expectations, and experiences.

The Graphic Organizer Report Assessment

Rubric

Rating Scale: 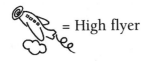 = High flyer   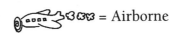 = Airborne   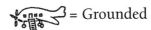 = Grounded

---

1. **Quality of Report Format:**
   The graphic organizer selected is an
   appropriate choice for use in the report.   Rating: _____

2. **Quality of Information:**
   The information shows significant research on the topic.   Rating: _____

3. **Grammar:**
   Spelling, grammar, and punctuation
   have been checked carefully.   Rating: _____

4. **Interest:**
   The different subtopics fit together well
   and highlight the main points of the topic.   Rating: _____

5. **Graphics/Creativity:**
   The graphic organizer fits the information to be
   organized and is used in a unique and/or creative way
   to convey the information as efficiently as possible.   Rating: _____

Comments by Student: _____

_____

_____

Signed _____ Date _____

Comments by Teacher: _____

_____

_____

Signed _____ Date _____

Overall Rating: _____

Signed _____ Date _____

Standards-Based LANGUAGE ARTS
Graphic Organizers & Rubrics for Elementary Students

Calendar for the Use of Graphic Organizers

	Monday	Tuesday	Wednesday	Thursday	Friday
Knowledge/ Comprehension	Use magazines, newspapers, and your textbooks to find a wide assortment of graphic organizers. State the main purpose or type of information given in each graphic organizer.	List all the different ways you can think of that we use graphic organizers in our everyday lives. Consider how they are used in department stores, in airports, in supermarkets, and in sports.	Define graphic organizers using your own words, then use a dictionary. Compare the two definitions.	Take the information in one of the graphic organizers and rewrite it in another form.	Classify your collection of graphic organizers in at least three different ways. Explain the rationale for your grouping.
Comprehension/ Application/ Analysis	Compare a chart and a table. In a good paragraph, summarize how they are alike and how they are different.	Collect information about junk foods popular with your age group. Use a Venn Diagram to show your results.	Construct a flowchart to show how you would like to spend a perfect 24-hour day.	Survey the students in your class to determine their favorite television show. Show your results on a graphic organizer.	How is a graphic organizer like a road map? Like a blueprint? Like a photograph?
Analysis/ Synthesis	Study your collection of graphic organizers. Determine some types of data and subject matter that are best depicted by a graphic organizer.	Diagram a flowchart for constructing a graph or a table on grade point averages for students in your language arts class.	Write a story that has one of the following titles: "The Magic Web" "Who Needs A Concept Map?" "Who Moved My Graphic Organizer?"	Draw a picture or write a paragraph to illustrate one of these expressions: "He turned the tables on me!" "It's time to chart your course!"	Design a poster about a school project, event, or activity that uses a graphic organizer as part of its message.
Evaluation	Develop a set of recommendations for students to follow when constructing a high-quality graphic organizer.	Develop a set of criteria for judging the worth or value of a given graphic organizer. Apply this criteria to each unit of your collection. Rank order your graphic organizers, from most effective to least effective.	Defend this statement: Presenting a graphic organizer is the best way to convince a friend of something.	Design a poster of graphic organizers. Find as many different examples as you can. Mount examples on poster board and write three insightful questions about each one.	Explain how each of the following people might use graphic organizers in their work: computer programmer, teacher, mall manager, astronaut, brain surgeon, and carpenter.

Standards-Based LANGUAGE ARTS
Graphic Organizers & Rubrics for Elementary Students

Gardner's Multiple Intelligences

Did you know there are eight different types of intelligence and that each of us possesses all eight, although one or more of them may be stronger than others? Dr. Howard Gardner, a researcher and professor at the Harvard Graduate School of Education, developed the Theory of Multiple Intelligences to help us better understand ourselves and the way we acquire information in school.

Try to rank order the eight intelligences below as they best describe the way *you* learn, with "1" being your weakest intelligence area and "8" being your strongest intelligence area. Try to think of examples and instances in the classroom when you were successful on a test, assignment, activity, or task because it was compatible with the way you like to learn.

_____ 1. **Linguistic Intelligence:** Do you find it easy to memorize information, write poems or stories, give oral talks, read books, play word games like Scrabble and Password, use big words in your conversations or assignments, and remember what you hear?

_____ 2. **Logical-Mathematical Intelligence:** Do you find it easy to compute numbers in your head and on paper, to solve brain teasers, to do logic puzzles, to conduct science experiments, to figure out number and sequence patterns, and to watch videos or television shows on science and nature themes?

_____ 3. **Spatial Intelligence:** Do you find it easy to draw, paint, or doodle, work through puzzles and mazes, build with blocks or various types of buildings sets, follow maps and flowcharts, use a camera to record what you see around you, and prefer reading material with many illustrations?

_____ 4. **Bodily-Kinesthetic Intelligence:** Do you find it easy to engage in lots of sports and physical activities, move around rather than sit still, spend free time outdoors, work with your hands on such things as model-building or sewing, participate in dance, ballet, gymnastics, plays, puppet shows or other performances, and mess around with finger painting, clay, and papier-maché?

_____ 5. **Musical Intelligence:** Do you find it easy to play a musical instrument or sing in the choir, listen to favorite records or tapes, make up your own songs or raps, recognize off-key recordings or noises, remember television jingles and lyrics of many different songs, and work while listening to or humming simple melodies and tunes?

_____ 6. **Interpersonal Intelligence:** Do you find it easy to make friends, meet strangers, resolve conflicts among peers, lead groups or clubs, engage in gossip, participate in team sports, plan social activities, and teach or counsel others?

_____ 7. **Intrapersonal Intelligence:** Do you find it easy to function independently, do your own work and thinking, spend time alone, engage in solo hobbies and activities, attend personal growth seminars, set goals, analyze your own strengths and weaknesses, and keep private diaries or journals?

_____ 8. **Naturalist Intelligence:** Do you find yourself extremely comfortable and happy outdoors, have a desire to explore and observe the environment, use outdoor equipment such as binoculars easily, and want to understand how natural systems evolve and how things work?

Bloom's Taxonomy of Cognitive Thinking Skills

Bloom's Taxonomy of Cognitive of Cognitive Thinking Skills is a model that can help you learn how to think critically and systematically. (*Taxonomy* is another word for *structure* or *schemata*.) This taxonomy provides a way to organize thinking skills into six levels. The first level is the most basic, or simplest, level of thinking, and the last level is the most challenging, or most complex, level of thinking.

KNOWLEDGE LEVEL:

Students thinking at this level are asked to memorize, remember, and recall previously learned material. Some common verbs or behaviors for this level are: define, list, identify, label, name, recall, record, draw, recite, and reproduce.

COMPREHENSION LEVEL:

Students thinking at this level are asked to demonstrate their ability to understand the meaning of material learned and to express that meaning in their own words. Some common verbs or behaviors for this level are: explain, describe, summarize, give examples, classify, find, measure, prepare, re-tell, reword, rewrite, and show.

APPLICATION LEVEL:

Students thinking at this level are asked to use learned material in a situation different from the situation in which the material was taught. Some common verbs or behaviors for this level are: apply, compute, construct, develop, discuss, generalize, interview, investigate, model, perform, plan, present, produce, prove, solve, and use.

ANALYSIS LEVEL:

Students thinking at this level are asked to break down material (ideas and concepts) into its component parts so that the organization and relationships between parts is better recognized and understood. Some common verbs or behaviors for this level are: compare and contrast, criticize, debate, determine, diagram, differentiate, discover, draw conclusions, examine, infer, search, survey, and sort.

SYNTHESIS LEVEL:

Students thinking at this level are asked to put together parts of the material to form a new and different whole. Synthesis is the exact opposite of analysis. Some common verbs or behaviors for this level are: build, combine, create, design, imagine, invent, make-up, produce, propose, and present.

EVALUATION LEVEL:

Students thinking at this level are asked to judge the value of material (a statement, novel, poem, research finding, fact) for a given purpose. All judgments are to be based on a set of clearly defined criteria whose outcomes can be defended or validated. Some common verbs or behaviors for this level are: assess, critique, defend, evaluate, grade, judge, measure, rank, recommend, select, test, validate, and verify.

Criteria for Creating Your Own Rubric

Excellent

My portfolio, project, or task
1. is complete.
2. is well-organized.
3. is visually exciting.
4. shows much evidence of multiple resources.
5. shows much evidence of problem solving, decision making, and higher-order thinking skills.
6. reflects enthusiasm for the subject.
7. contains additional work beyond the requirements.
8. communicates effectively what I have learned in keeping with my learning objectives.
9. includes highly efficient assessment tools and makes ample provisions for meta-cognitive reflection.
10. has identified many future learning goals in keeping with my own needs and interests.

Good

My portfolio, project, or task
1. is complete.
2. is well-organized.
3. is interesting.
4. shows some evidence of multiple resources.
5. shows some evidence of problem solving, decision making, and higher-order thinking skills.
6. reflects some interest for the topic.
7. contains a small amount of work beyond the requirements.
8. communicates some things I have learned in keeping with my learning objectives.
9. includes effective assessment tools and reflective comments.
10. has identified some future learning goals in keeping with my own needs and interests.

Needs Improvement

My portfolio, project, or task
1. is incomplete.
2. is poorly organized.
3. is not very interesting to others.
4. shows little or almost no evidence of multiple resources.
5. shows little or almost no evidence of problem solving, decision making, and higher-order thinking skills.
6. reflects little interest in the subject.
7. contains no additional work beyond the minimum requirements.
8. communicates few things that I have truly learned in keeping with my objectives.
9. includes few examples of self assessment tools and reflective comments.
10. has identified no future learning goals in keeping with my own needs and interests.

Standards-Based LANGUAGE ARTS
Graphic Organizers & Rubrics for Elementary Students

Performance, Project, or Task
Independent Study Contract

Title _____

Topic _____

Beginning date of work_____

Planned completion/delivery date _____

Goals and/or learning objectives to be accomplished_____

_____

Statement of problems to be researched/studied _____

_____

Format _____

Information/data/resources needed _____

_____

Technical help needed_____

_____

Special equipment and/or materials needed _____

_____

Visual aids and/or artifacts planned_____

_____

Intended audience_____

Method of assessment_____

Student Signature _____ Date: _____

Teacher Signature _____ Date: _____

Standards-Based LANGUAGE ARTS
Graphic Organizers & Rubrics for Elementary Students

BIBLIOGRAPHY
of
Related Incentive Publications Products

Basic/Not Boring, Grades K-1:
    by Imogene Forte and Marjorie Frank
    Language Arts Topics in—*Phonics & Word Recognition; Reading; Language, Writing, & Usage*

Basic/Not Boring, Grades 2-3:
    by Imogene Forte and Marjorie Frank
    Language Arts Topics in—*Phonics & Word Skills; Reading; Language, Writing, & Usage; Spelling*

Basic/Not Boring, Grades 4-5:
    by Imogene Forte and Marjorie Frank
    Language Arts Topics in—*Reading Comprehension; Grammar & Usage; Words & Vocabulary; Writing, Spelling, Study & Research*

Book-A-Brations!
    by Jan Grubb Philpot

Book-A-Tivities!
    by Jan Grubb Philpot

Celebrate with Books
    by Imogene Forte and Joy MacKenzie

Complete Writing Lessons for the Primary Grades
    by Marjorie Frank

Curriculum and Project Planner for Integrating Learning Styles, Thinking Skills, and Authentic Assessment, Revised Edition
    by Imogene Forte and Sandra Schurr

ESL Content-Based Language Games, Puzzles, and Inventive Exercises
    by Imogene Forte and Mary Ann Pangle

(continued)

Standards-Based LANGUAGE ARTS
Graphic Organizers & Rubrics for Elementary Students

ESL Reading and Spelling Games, Puzzles, and Inventive Exercises
  by Imogene Forte and Mary Ann Pangle

ESL Vocabulary and Word Usage Games, Puzzles, and Inventive Exercises
  by Imogene Forte and Mary Ann Pangle

ESL Active Learning Lessons
  by Imogene Forte and Mary Ann Pangle

If You're Trying to Teach Kids How to Write, You've Gotta Have This Book, Rev. Ed.
  by Marjorie Frank

Internet Adventures for Young Children
  by Catherine H. Cook and Janet M. Pfeifer

Internet Quest
  by Catherine H. Cook and Janet M. Pfeifer

The Kids' Stuff™ Book of Reading and Language Arts, Primary
  by Imogene Forte and Joy MacKenzie

Language Literacy Lessons in Reading
  by Imogene Forte

Language Literacy Lessons in Words & Vocabulary
  by Imogene Forte

Language Literacy Lessons in Writing
  by Imogene Forte

Learning Through Research
  by Shirley Cook

Linking Literature & Comprehension
  by Shirley Cook

On the Loose with Dr. Seuss
  by Shirley Cook

Selling Spelling to Kids, Revised Edition
  by Imogene Forte and Mary Ann Pangle

INDEX

Standards-Based LANGUAGE ARTS
Graphic Organizers & Rubrics for Elementary Students